THE
Divine Life
OF
Animals

THE
Divine Life
OF
Animals

ONE MAN'S QUEST TO
DISCOVER WHETHER THE
SOULS OF ANIMALS LIVE ON

Ptolemy Tompkins

CROWN PUBLISHERS

NEW YORK

Grateful acknowledgment is made to the following for permission to reprint previously published material:

Cengage Learning/Nelson Education: Excerpt from "The Lord of Animals" by Otto Zerries in *The Encyclopedia of Religion.*

Guideposts magazine: Excerpt from "The Man Who Rescues Manatees" by Deke Beusse, copyright © 2000 by Guideposts, Guideposts.com. All rights reserved. Reprinted by permission of *Guideposts* magazine.

HarperCollins Publishers: Excerpt from *Kinship with All Life* by J. Allen Boone, copyright © 1954 by Harper & Brothers, copyright renewed © 1982 by Daniel U. Boone, Jr., and Lois Boone Ragsdale. Reprinted by permission of HarperCollins Publishers.

Hyperion Books: Excerpt from *Summers with the Bears* by Jack Becklund, copyright © 1999 by Jack Becklund.

The Parapsychology Foundation, Inc.: Excerpt from *Adventures in the Supernormal* by Eileen J. Garrett, copyright © 2002 by Eileen Coly.

Pantheon Books: Excerpt from "Why Look at Animals?" from *About Looking* by John Berger, copyright © 1980 by John Berger. Reprinted by permission of Pantheon Books, a division of Random House, Inc.

Penguin Books, Ltd.: Excerpt from *Gilgamesh*, translated by N. K. Sandars, copyright © 1960, 1964, 1972 by N. K. Sandars. Reprinted by permission of Penguin Books, Ltd.

Copyright © 2010 by Ptolemy Tompkins

Published in the United States by Crown Publishers, an imprint of the Crown Publishing Group, a division of Random House, Inc., New York.
www.crownpublishing.com

CROWN and the Crown colophon are registered trademarks of Random House, Inc.

Library of Congress Cataloging-in-Publication Data

Tompkins, Ptolemy.
The divine life of animals : one man's quest to discover whether the souls of animals live on / Ptolemy Tompkins.—1st ed.
p.   cm.
Includes bibliographical references and index.
1. Pets—Miscellanea.   2. Soul—Miscellanea.   3. Future life—Miscellanea.
4. Pets—Death—Miscellanea.   I. Title.
BF1999.T625 2010
133.901'3—dc22
2009048597

ISBN 978-0-307-45132-3

Printed in the United States of America

Design by Chris Welch

1 3 5 7 9 10 8 6 4 2

First Edition

For Francie

CONTENTS

AUTHOR'S NOTE

Many people disapprove of calling a people, practice, or belief "primitive" these days, on the grounds that the word smacks of antiquated beliefs about the superiority of modern Western culture and the inferiority of peoples less technologically "advanced" (another tricky word). I, however, have always liked the sound and feel of *primitive*, and dislike the idea that just because it was used poorly for a while it now can't be used at all. In what follows, it should be kept in mind that, of its several dictionary meanings, I generally intend its first ("of or relating to an earliest or original stage or state; primeval") rather than its second ("characterized by simplicity or crudity; unsophisticated").

This book started out with the working title *The Divine Life of Pets*, but shifted to its current one after I noticed two things: first, it's really not "pets" I'm talking about, but all animals; second, even if I were just talking about pets, the word would still be best left out of the title, as *pet* is becoming, in our politically conscious world, ever more of a loaded term. *Animal companion* is fast becoming the favored term for a domesticated animal kept for pleasure rather than utility, and while I see the logic of this switch, the term doesn't always flow easily off the tongue—or onto my computer screen for that matter. Consequently, while removing it from the title, I've chosen to keep the word *pets* in my text. All the same, the impetus behind the move away from the word *pet* is, as I try to show in the story I tell here, a laudable one. It acknowledges what every pet owner knows: that the animals we keep are not possessions but fellow travelers on our life's journey, and it is precisely by being both (a) animals and (b) companions that they perform a dual service: not only are they our friends, but they are links back to a time when the shape and character of that journey was very different than it is now. As the novelist Milan Kundera wrote, in a passage that (if we substitute animals at large for dogs) could serve as a fitting epigraph for this entire book: "Dogs are our link to paradise. They don't know evil or jealousy or discontent. To sit with a dog on a hillside on a glorious afternoon is to be back in Eden, where doing nothing was not boring—it was peace."

THE
Divine Life
OF
Animals

INTRODUCTION

The eyes of an animal have the capacity of a great
language.

—Martin Buber (1878–1965)

The world is well supplied with interesting books about animals. Some focus on animal behavior. Some discuss the complex—and often controversial—subject of animals and ethics: how we should behave toward our fellow creatures, what rights they do or don't have, and what responsibilities we humans have toward them as a result. Others discuss the fascinating subject of communication between humans and animals: whether certain nonhuman creatures possess at least the rudiments of language, and what possibilities there might be for genuine communication between them and us if they do.

This book isn't about any of those things. I can think of no better way to explain what it *is* about than to tell the story of a small white dog that I met on the Yucatán Peninsula in the fall of 1974.

I was twelve at the time, tagging along with my father while he, my stepmother, and two other friends toured the region as part of the research my father was doing for a book on its ancient pyramid cultures. Pyramids and temples interested me not in the least at that age, and while the adults around me focused their attentions on one ancient pile of rocks after another, I looked for animals.

Most children like animals to some degree, but there's a certain kind of young person who does more than just like them: he identifies with them. For this latter kind of child, animals are more consequential, more congenial—and in certain ways at least, more *real* than humans are. If childhood is a period in which we are coaxed, willingly or otherwise, out of a state of natural innocence and into a state of acculturation to the human condition, animal-oriented children have a larger-than-average suspicion of this transition. For them the trade of animal innocence for human knowledge is one that's quite simply not worth making.

That was the kind of kid I was. So while the cultural aspects of my father's Yucatán adventure left me decidedly indifferent on that trip, the sea and jungle and the creatures that filled them gave me plenty of reason to be glad I'd been brought along all the same.

Not that all the animals I encountered were all that alien or exotic. In fact, the first ones I usually saw in each new town or city we visited were dogs. They were everywhere: hovering at the fringes of the outdoor restaurants where we ate, lounging in the courtyards of the hotels—hungry, obsequious, and always ready to bolt at the first sudden motion from a human.

Though few people seemed to be interested in doing so, these dogs were easy to win over if you cared to try. Approaching them slowly and holding out my hand, I'd find that all but the most skittish would soon start wagging their tails and crowding around, overjoyed—or so it seemed to me—that someone was at last paying them a little attention. It didn't hurt if you had some food to offer as well, and in more than one of the endless string of hotels we stayed in, my father, looking around for some bag of restaurant leftovers he'd set aside, would learn with irritation that I had parceled it out to whatever particular set of dogs were camped outside.

On the day in question we got up early and took a two-hour jeep ride to a set of ruins deep in the jungle. Near the ruins were a small group of huts, one of which had a generator-powered cooler full of soda and beer, and a grubby but serviceable snack counter. Lounging in front of the counter was the usual handful of dogs. My eye immediately fell on one of them—a singularly small, singularly pathetic-looking white female that didn't look like she was more than a few months old. Thumping her bony tail in the dust as I approached, she responded to my outstretched hand with tentative, sheepish, but scarcely concealed excitement. *At last,* her look seemed to say, *someone's noticed I'm here.*

This dog, who I christened Penny in honor of a single small copper-colored spot on her shoulder, followed along as we toured the temples, her tail swinging with such enthusiasm that it kept threatening to topple her over. Penny was so painfully thin that I decided I'd give her an extra-large portion of my lunch when we were back at the storefront.

Once we got there, however, my stepmother read my mind.

"Ptolly," she said as one of our guides handed me a plate of tortillas, chicken, and beans, "don't feed that dog."

"Why not?"

"Because it's not respectful to the people who live here. They have little enough as it is, and it's rude to throw food away right in front of them."

"Giving food to a dog isn't throwing it away," I said acidly.

"It is when you're in a country like this," my stepmother said. "You can't get emotionally attached to every animal you see down here. It isn't realistic."

Before we could get any further in our conversation, one of the guides came over and—not with excessive care but not roughly, either—swept Penny up in his hand and set her down behind a low wire fence enclosing a few scraggly chickens. Smiling what seemed to me a genuine smile (rather than the phony-friendly one that I noticed a lot of the natives gave the rich visiting gringos) he said something to us in Spanish—too quickly for me to understand.

"What did he say?" I asked my stepmother.

"He said don't worry about feeding that dog. It won't live more than a few days anyhow."

It was a strange moment: one in which four different perspectives on the world (mine, my stepmother's, the guide's, and last but not least, Penny's) met and faced off, like cars at a prairie intersection. *Realistic*: Just what, I wondered, did this word really mean? I knew that my stepmother was accurate in suggesting that I'd picked Penny out of a world of possible creatures to feel sorry for—that my near-instant emotional attachment to her was somewhat arbitrary. Moreover, the plate of food I was pondering giving to Penny was made up, in part, of chickens that no doubt had recently been chasing each other around the dirt just like the still-living ones before me now were. What about them? And—now that one had gotten on that tack—what of the cows that had furnished the leather of the shoes I was wearing? The first inklings of a vast, confusing, and exhausting universe of animal-rights issues spread itself out just about anywhere I looked, and just because Penny was more endearing than a chicken, more vulnerable-looking than a cow, that did not mean it was necessarily correct of me to elevate her to a status of greater importance than them.

But Penny and I had connected. I had looked into her face and seen something there—something that made me want to give her a name, and that had raised her instantly and irreversibly out of the realm of abstraction. The "emotional attachment" I'd struck up with Penny made her, in my eyes at least, more real than everything else around us. And if ignoring that fact, if eating my lunch right in front of her while pretending she didn't exist, was the kind of realism the adult world demanded of me, then the adults were welcome to their realism. I'd stick with my own brand.

I walked over to the fence and looked down at Penny. Tail wagging and oblivious to my stepmother's and the guide's comments, she continued to stare up at me with that same wild look of hope—only slightly diminished now by the wire that separated us. It was a look that, I suddenly realized, I was starting to hate. I hated it because every time I saw it in the faces of the dogs I met down here in this picturesque but somehow horrible place, I was doomed to disappoint them. Beyond a pat on the head and a few scraps of food, what did I really have to give these animals? Not a thing. When I left—in fact, the instant

I turned my gaze away from them—they went right back to being what they had been before I arrived: mere things on the periphery of a world full of other, much more important things.

I waited till my stepmother and the guide had turned their attentions elsewhere, then picked a large piece of chicken from my plate and dropped it in the dirt in front of Penny. As she wolfed it down, I turned and walked away.

My father had seen what he needed to see of the site, and with lunch done we climbed into the jeep and started the long, bumping ride back to the hotel. Staring out at the jungle flashing past, I watched for birds and other interesting animals, and did what I could to push Penny out of my head.

But she wouldn't go. Not completely at least. Thirty-some years later, in fact, she's still there: a dime-a-dozen, parasite-infested, little white mongrel dog staring up at me over a crummy wire fence, her tail going a mile a minute, her expression full of hope and the promise—if not the actuality—of happiness.

In the years since that day, I've become a member in good standing of that worldly-wise adult community which, back when I was twelve, I had such ambivalent feelings about joining. I have a job, a mortgage, and as solid a grasp of what can and can't be expected from life as my stepmother could ever have wanted me to. In short, I've learned how to be realistic.

But that hasn't prevented me, every now and then, from asking myself certain unrealistic questions—and it's when I do so that Penny is most likely to come to mind. What, exactly, *was* Penny in the end? When, as surely happened, she died a few days or weeks after I last saw her, what remained of her beyond the few negligible pounds of fur and flesh that had made up her physical body? What, to get even more specific, became of that sparkle of hope (for as decidedly human as that word is, it is still, I believe, the only correct name to give it) that I'd seen so clearly in her eyes? Did it vanish completely, or was there something— some infinitely mysterious nonmaterial core of *Penny-ness*—that did not disappear when she breathed her last?

For many people, of course, these kinds of questions sound more than unrealistic; they sound outright absurd: the soft-hearted, sentimental, screamingly anthropomorphic fantasies of someone unable—or unwilling—to see the world as it actually is. But is the world as it actually is really the cruel, final, and unforgivingly one-dimensional place it (admittedly) so often seems to be? Or is there another part of the world—a part we don't see most of the time, but of which we catch a glimpse when we establish even the briefest of connections with another living creature? "At the center of our being," wrote Thomas Merton in a celebrated passage, "is a point of pure truth, a point or spark which belongs entirely to God. . . . It is like a pure diamond blazing with the invisible light of heaven. It is in everybody, and if we could see it, we would see these billions of points of light coming together in the face and blaze of a sun that would make all the darkness and cruelty of life vanish completely."

Merton was talking about people here, not animals. But in spite of this, he surely would not have disagreed with the idea that behind the look that that small white dog gave me from behind that chicken-wire fence that day in the Yucatán there lay a genuine being. A being that, though perhaps not in the exact manner of *human* beings, blazed with the invisible light of heaven all the same.

Penny, then, must have had a soul.

Wait a minute. A *soul*? Even when they're not sure exactly why, most people sense that to connect the word *soul* to the word *animal* is to stray onto dangerous ground—to call up old and no doubt tediously complicated arguments between the kinds of people (Greek philosophers, medieval Church fathers) who were more than ready to put aside whole sections of their day to chewing over such matters.

These dry and dusty arguments do indeed exist—plenty of them—but we don't have to be philosophy professors to understand the basic questions that define most of them. That's because these questions come to us by themselves, usually at a very early age. A friend of mine once told me that the first genuine distinction her daughter learned to make as a young child came when she was watching a colony of ants that had invaded their upstairs bathroom. "Moving," said the girl, pointing to one ant hurriedly making its way across the white linoleum. "Not moving," she said of another ant—a dead one—that lay off and away from the rest.

That moving/not-moving distinction is the birthplace of all soul philosophies. *Move* derives from the same root that gives us the word *emotion*. Things that move physically—animate beings—share a bond with us, and when those things stop moving, something deep inside us recognizes and responds to that loss. "Where did it go?" children often say when the living body of an animal or insect suddenly goes still. It's this strange disappearance, this vanishing of the mysterious "it" that made the animal or insect body move, that makes us first realize that the physical body in and of itself—this thing that moves for a while and then stops moving once and for all—cannot be all there is to the picture: that there must be something more.

In many languages, the word for *soul* is the same as the word for *breath*. *Nephesh*, for example, the closest equivalent to *soul* in the Hebrew Bible, is what God breathes into the nose of Adam after he has molded him from the clay of Eden. Throughout Genesis and later on in the Bible as well, the word can connote either physical breath, immaterial spirit, or both at once. As R. B. Onians, professor of Latin at the University of London, points out, *nephesh* "is clearly something in man (or any other animal) which is necessary to life and with which life is closely bound up. So Michal, David's wife, told him: 'If thou save not thy *nephesh* tonight, tomorrow thou shalt be slain.' "

Nephesh in its spiritual sense is not, however, some generic, nonmaterial juice that powers us the way electricity powers a robot. It's more personal than that. Indeed, our *nephesh* is what makes each of us *who we are*. As Professor Onians writes, it's "the chief designation of the conscious self."

Blood—that other most important life-sustaining substance—is connected with soul almost as inseparably in the ancient world as breath is. The English *soul* comes from the Anglo-Saxon *sawol*, which like the Hebrew *nephesh*, the Latin *anima*, and the Greek *psyche*, hooks up frequently in the ancient mind not just with breath and movement, but with blood as well. Spilled blood, if the air around it is cold enough, gives off steam, and in the *Iliad* and other ancient texts where copious blood is spilled, the departing soul-stuff often takes a foglike or steamlike form. Going back to Genesis, Abel's blood could cry from the ground after it was spilled by his brother Cain because that blood still carried his actual, personal life-essence—his Abel-ness—within it.

Anima is also the root of the word *animal*, and the idea that humans alone possess a soul or spirit that goes elsewhere when the body dies would not have made much—or any—sense to the archaic mind. When, in the lines quoted above, Professor Onians describes *nephesh* as inhering in man "or any other animal," he is not saying anything that an ancient Hebrew would have disagreed with. For though humans stand apart in the Bible as uniquely inspired examples of God's handiwork, they are not in any fundamental way removed from the rest of creation because of this.

At least they weren't until something went wrong. It is with the Fall, and only with the Fall, that Adam and Eve first sense that they are somehow set apart from animals, and from the rest of creation as well. Not coincidentally, this is also the moment when death first enters the picture—the same death that, when we discover it as children, alerts us that something is somehow amiss with the life we have been born into down here in the world.

What happens to a child, how does he or she react, after the where-did-it-go question has been asked? Stephen Webb, in his book *Of God and Dogs*, tells the story of something that happened to him as a very young child—so young, in fact, that he only knows the details because his mother described them to him later. "We were in a post office," Webb writes, "and she [his mother] turned away from me for a moment, only to be startled by loud cries that she knew were mine. When she found me, a woman apologized to her, explaining that she had accidentally stepped on a ladybug that I had been following across the floor, and that had sent me into tears."

Here's another story. "Many years ago," a friend of mine wrote me recently, "my four-year-old son and I were watching a TV documentary about seals. The way I remember it, the seal family was swimming happily around in the icy water, when some humans came along and killed the mother. The baby seal swam over, taking in the terrible new situation. Seeing this, my normally quiet, calm little son went to pieces. 'Why?' he asked, 'is the baby seal crying?' He must have seen lots of TV death by then, but it was as if the horror of death suddenly hit him for the first time."

Most of us can conjure up a memory like this. It's the moment when we as individuals reenact what Genesis describes happening to humankind at large: the moment when we fell away from that initial state of simplicity and innocence where we had lived as one with nature, into a world that is no longer either simple or innocent or, unfortunately, entirely good.

"Children often identify with animals in ways that amuse and frustrate us," Webb writes about his memory of the ladybug in the post office, "spending emotion with an abandon that adults, with their thrifty investments and prudent decisions, cannot afford."

It was, of course, precisely that impractical abandon that my stepmother was trying to warn me about that day down in the Yucatán. And on one level she was absolutely right. If any of us walked through life in a state of genuine childlike openness to the dramas that unfold around us—on either the animal or the human level—few of us would make it to lunch without being destroyed by them completely.

But even if we have no choice but to adapt ourselves to the

rules of life as we find them down here in the world of the moving/not-moving—the fallen world of alienation and loss and hard, cold, adult practicality—that doesn't mean the story necessarily comes to a halt with this accommodation. And just as animals are always present in stories of the fall out of original innocence (be they of an entire people in distant centuries past, or of a single child playing on the floor of a post office), so, too, are they present when people speak of the unfallen realms of spirit that we may someday once again find and reenter.

In what is probably the single best-known passage of writing about our relationship to nonhuman creation written in the last century, the naturalist Henry Beston wrote that

> we need another and a wiser and perhaps a more mystical concept of animals. Remote from universal nature, and living by complicated artifice, man in civilization surveys the creature through the glass of his knowledge and sees thereby a feather magnified and the whole image in distortion. We patronize them for their incompleteness, for their tragic fate of having taken form so far below ourselves. And therein we err, and greatly err. For the animal shall not be measured by man. In a world older and more complete than ours they move finished and complete, gifted with extensions of the senses we have lost or never attained, living by voices we shall never hear. They are not brethren, they are not underlings; they are other nations, caught with ourselves in the net of life and time, fellow prisoners of the splendor and travail of the earth.

Though of course I didn't have the sophistication to voice it in anything like those terms, that "more mystical concept of animals"—that wise-yet-innocent manner of looking at non-human creation—was precisely what I was obscurely groping for that day when I met Penny. There had to be a way of coming to grips with our mutual situation as earthly creatures that was realistic—that stood up to the adult world with its adult meanings—but that nonetheless allowed me to acknowledge that glint of immortality I saw so clearly in her eyes.

That new-yet-old vision—that recovery of a way of understanding animals that will allow us to see them as the genuine soul-beings they are and always have been—is what *this* particular book on animals is all about.

Mystery

A Little Man in a Bunny Suit

At the age of twenty-four, on a whim, I became the owner of a Netherlands dwarf bunny named Angus. Physically, Angus was about the size of a softball, but in terms of personality he soon established himself as considerably larger. My then-girlfriend Sarah and I moved around a lot in those days, but wherever we went, Angus went with us. Whether I was waiting tables in Massachusetts, working as an office temp in New York, or finishing the manuscript of my first book in a beach apartment in San Diego (ironically enough, on those same ancient Mesoamerican pyramid cultures that I'd found so boring at age twelve), Angus was always there, ready to cheer Sarah and me up with his quirky little repertoire of habits. When he was feeling feisty, Angus would charge back and forth and thump his back feet on the floor. In more-relaxed moments, he'd stretch himself out on his side like a cat—something neither Sarah nor I had ever known rabbits did. Sometimes, waking up from a nap on our futon, I'd find him perched—alertly as usual—on my head.

Up to that point, my experiences with small, warm-blooded pets had been confined to gerbils, mice, and guinea pigs. These animals were fine as far as they went, but there was, I had learned, only so much that could be expected from them personality-wise. When I first brought Angus home, I'd had no great expectations from him in this department, either. He was, I figured, simply about as much of a pet as Sarah and I, given how much we moved around and how little an idea we had of what we were doing with our lives, could handle.

But right from the start, Angus proved me wrong. Though most of what he did was indeed very predictable and clearly directed by instinct—that basic Rabbit 1.0 operating system that he, like every other member of his tribe, came into the world possessing—he went about these activities with a certain unmistakable individuality—one might even say a *style*.

You could see this individual spin Angus put on his rabbit behaviors in all kinds of places—from the curiously nonchalant way he had of holding a stalk of alfalfa with his front paws as he munched his way down it, to the ever so slight but unmistakable look of bemusement he would get on his face sometimes when he was just sitting around. Just a rabbit? No way. Angus was *Angus*.

Through a Human Lens

Not that these qualities appeared with such clarity to everyone else. "I can't believe the way you two anthropomorphize that animal," my best friend Greg—a chemist's son with a considerable knowledge of science—would say as he watched us fussing over our tiny surrogate child. "Do you know how big his brain is?" (Matters were not helped in this regard by Sarah's habit of calling Angus her "little man," as she would every morning when she let Angus out of his cage with a cheery "And how's my little man today?")

I knew Greg was right—at least technically. Sarah and I did load Angus down with a little more in the way of human qualities than he was capable of carrying. But that was what people had always done, right? All you had to do to see that was look in a medieval bestiary, with its wildly unrealistic drawings of animals, accompanied by long lists of their Christian virtues and vices, or open one of the books on mythology that I kept lined up on the floor next to our futon for consultation while writing my book on ancient Mesoamerica. An illustration in one of these books—a translation of the *Popol Vuh,* the sacred book of the Quiche Maya Indians of Guatemala—always made me think of Angus in particular. The illustration was from an ancient Mayan ceremonial vase, and featured a creature with a rabbit's head and a human body dressed in Maya garb and crouched, pen in hand, over a ceremonial jaguar-skin scroll. "Rabbit scribe," said the caption below this figure—summing up in two words the basic nature of the human attitude toward animals since time immemorial. When they looked at animals, people never saw them as they really and truly were. Whether it be thick or thin, dirty or clean, we humans always looked at animals through a lens: the lens of our humanity. Even scientifically minded people like Greg, I suspected, didn't see the actual animal when they looked at a creature like Angus, but rather a furry little robot: a residue from the early, ultra-mechanistic days of modern science when all of nature was seen as one big, dead, empty machine. From primitive tribes to medieval peasants to modern scientists, *no one* saw animals with total clarity. So who could blame Sarah and me if we too indulged in a little of this kind of creative license with our curiously personable pet rabbit?

An Unfair Fight

In addition to the other uncertainties in our life, Sarah and I would sometimes argue and break off our relationship for periods. During one of these separations, she moved out to San Diego with Angus while I stayed behind, back East. I was halfway through my book on Mesoamerica when, over the phone, we decided to get back together again. In the spring of 1989, I loaded up my car with my bulky second-rate computer and all my boxes of myth-and-religion books and joined her out West.

By the time I showed up at the ratty if pleasant Pacific Beach apartment Sarah had rented just twelve blocks from the ocean, Angus was having issues with his new place of residence. Specifically, he had developed a flea problem.

"He's so small," Sarah would say as Angus came to an abrupt halt in the middle of the brown shag carpet in the living room and started scratching himself furiously. "It's not a fair fight."

Sarah went to the vet and got some flea shampoo, and from then on Angus received regular baths in our kitchen sink. Angus hated these baths, and Sarah and I didn't like giving them to him, either. There was something about the way the water *reduced* Angus—taking away his absurdly fluffy, cuddly, children's-book rabbitness and transforming him into a wet, squirming, ungainly creature with oversized back feet and a racing heart—that brought both of us up short. Angus, we'd realize in such moments, was indeed neither a little machine nor a little man in a bunny suit. But he very definitely *was* a mortal creature—one that was destined to be with us for only a limited amount of time.

So it went for several months. We'd towel Angus off and

send him back about his business, and for a while the scratching would stop. But then it would start up again, and we'd have to put him back under the tap for another noxious bath. Sometimes, in addition to the scratching, Angus would be overcome with short but violent fits of sneezing. Other times he'd lie sluggishly, refusing to hop and stomp around for days at a time. We took him to the vet, but other than advising us to keep him extra warm right after his baths, they couldn't tell us anything.

That fall, I finally finished my book on ancient Mesoamerica and sent it off to the publisher. To celebrate, I invited Greg out from the East Coast for a visit. One day during this visit, he, Sarah, and I went down to spend the day just across the border in Tijuana. We got back to the apartment in the early evening and found a cloth draped over Angus's cage. A note from our roommate Cindy, who worked the morning and evening shifts at a restaurant, lay on top.

"Dear Sarah and Ptolemy," the note read, "please prepare yourselves before you look in Angus's cage. When I got home today he was no longer alive."

I lifted the cloth, and there was Sarah's and my little ball of personality lying on his side, stock-still.

A Quarrel in Paradise

In an essay called "Why Look at Animals?" the novelist and critic John Berger quotes a story from the Nuer people of the Southern Sudan about how the present world came into being. All creatures including man, says this story, "originally lived together in fellowship in one camp. Dissension began after Fox persuaded Mongoose to throw a club into Elephant's face. A quarrel ensued and the animals separated; each went its own way and began to live as they now are, and to kill each other. Stomach, which at first lived a life of its own in the bush, entered into man so that now he is always hungry. The sexual organs, which had also been separate, attached themselves to men and women, causing them to desire one another constantly. Elephant taught man how to pound millet so that now he satisfies his hunger only by ceaseless labor. Mouse taught man to beget and woman to bear. And Dog brought fire to man."

Something about this myth of human and animal origins had struck me with particular vividness when I'd first read it several years before—right around the time Angus had come into our lives. I liked the way it described the loss of direct kinship between humans and animals in practically the same breath as it described an implicit drop down out of a world of pure spirit. I also liked the emphasis on the fact that *need* had entered into the world along with this drop: the need to work and to procreate, the need for one group of animals to prey upon another, the need to kill and to avoid being killed. On the package of Angus's favorite brand of pet snack—a stick made of compressed seeds—there was a cartoon that always amused Sarah and me. A rabbit and a guinea pig were pictured chipping away at one of the snack sticks with pickaxes. "They must work for every bite," said the caption. "That is nature's way." That did indeed seem to sum things up. Struggle and strife, work and death: these were the fundamental realities faced by every creature that was born into this hardscrabble physical world of ours.

Or were they? For though the cartoon suggested that pets

like Angus needed to work and struggle to earn their keep just as other animals did, there was no denying that a life like Angus's contained considerably less in this department than it would have if he had been born a wild rabbit. This was, of course, because Angus was a pet, and pets, since the very beginnings of human culture, have lived by a different set of rules than other animals.

Pets, Old and New

"In the past," wrote Berger in that same essay which included the Nuer myth, "families of all classes kept domestic animals because they served a useful purpose—guard dogs, hunting dogs, mice-killing cats, and so on. The practice of keeping animals regardless of their usefulness, the keeping, exactly of *pets* (in the sixteenth century the word usually referred to a lamb raised by hand) is a modern innovation, and, on the social scale on which it exists today, is unique."

Berger, in this passage, makes it seem like the pet concept was invented very recently, but this is an arguable point. The ancient Egyptians kept pet baboons, gazelles, and of course cats in abundance, and often had them mummified so that a particularly beloved animal could keep its master company in the land of the dead. (It should be pointed out, however, that a mummified dog or cat was not always evidence that the animal within enjoyed a particularly intimate relationship with its human owner. The Egyptians mummified their animals not only to serve as companions in the afterlife but also as sacrifices to their huge pantheon of gods. In the later days of Egyptian civilization, the custom became a rote affair in which animal mummies sold in temples didn't even necessarily hold whole animals, but a sausagelike mix from different ones.) The women of ancient Rome were as keen about their small dogs as any Upper East Side New York matron is today, and there are plentiful indications that Stone Age humanity possessed at least the rudiments of the pet concept. A burial in the Neolithic Natufian village of 'Ain Mallaha, near the shores of the Mediterranean, for example, yielded the remains of an elderly person tenderly cradling a young dog.

The pets of centuries past by and large existed, however, in a world much less insulated than ours from the dog-eat-dog realities that held for their fellow non-pet animals. After all, precious few humans were able to keep themselves distanced from the harsh exigencies of physical existence back then, so it seems unlikely that they would have been able to provide this luxury to their companion animals.

In the course of researching my book on Mesoamerica, I'd encountered countless examples of how much harsher and more uncompromising the human-animal relationship had been in times past than it is now, and how much less likely an ancient pet owner would be to coddle an animal and protect it from the nastiness of life the way good pet owners are expected to do today. One fact that struck me in particular was that certain monkey-eating tribes in the jungles of both the Old World and New World often kept the babies of mother monkeys they killed in the hunt and raised them as beloved village mascots. To befriend a creature whose mother one has killed and eaten sounds grotesque to the average animal-loving member of the modern world, but for most of history (and all of prehistory) this kind of hairsplitting was an unaffordable luxury. "A peasant," wrote Berger, "becomes fond of his pig and is glad to salt away its pork. What is significant, and is so difficult for the urban stranger to understand, is that the two statements in the sentence are connected by an *and* and not by a *but.*"

I knew very well whom Berger meant by the term *urban stranger.* He meant people so thoroughly and hopelessly distanced from the brute facts of existence in the material world that they allowed themselves to forget, ninety-nine percent of the time, that they relied on the toil and the lives of animals with practically every move they made. In other words, he was talking about Sarah and me. Despite our amusement at that cartoon of the hard-working rabbit and guinea pig on the package of Angus's snack sticks, the fact was that we really didn't want Angus to play a part in the real world: the world of predators and victims, of beasts that eat and beasts that are eaten—of creatures who (to speak in mythic terms), though formerly clothed in pure spirit, were now reduced to endlessly stealing one another's flesh in order that their physical bodies could survive. He was too lovable for that! So like countless other pet owners, we excused Angus from having to do so, half-secretly hoping that the rules of life and death that applied out there in the rest of the world would simply never touch him.

A Rabbit Laid to Rest

And guess what? It worked! In our care, Angus had become a textbook example of the modern pet: a creature kept at such a complete remove from all the nastier aspects of life in the material world that it was almost as if he still lived in paradise: that carefree place where (as the Nuer myth had put it) humans and animals had all dwelled happily in the same camp, and no one ever had to kill or otherwise prey upon another because no one yet had a physical body to maintain.

At least until those accursed fleas had come along.

There wasn't much in the way of grass around the beach house, so Sarah and I wrapped Angus in his favorite blue felt blanket, put him in a shoebox, and drove to Sarah's mother's more properly suburban house several miles inland. Her mom found a shovel in the garage, and I poked around in the corner of the yard for a spot that was free of buried pipes or wires. Then, with the sun sinking low in the cloudless, anemic-looking Southern California sky, I dug a hole. When it was deep enough, I took Angus from the shoebox and laid him—still wrapped in his blanket—in the earth. Once I'd covered it over again, a still-tearful Sarah knelt and placed a rock on top of it, painted (in Wite-Out borrowed from my desk back at the beach house) with the word ANGUS and the small, simple outline of a heart.

Standing behind Sarah with her mother and a fidgety Greg (who, despite his equivocal feelings about the size of Angus's brain, was doing his best to accommodate to the sudden tragic turn his visit had taken), I found myself doing what mourners at funerals always do: meditating on the life of the deceased, and seeing it for the first time ever as a story with a beginning, a middle . . . and an end.

In particular, I couldn't stop thinking about how strangely dignified Angus had looked when we'd first discovered him lying dead in his cage. I'd noticed this look in dead animals before—often in very unlikely places. A white-tailed deer killed by a car lying by the side of the road in West Virginia; a harbor seal washed up on a Maine beach—even animals hanging in butcher-shop windows could have it. It was as if the animal's body had become an emblem of its departed soul's transformation into something larger, stranger, and more remote than what it had been in life.

For archaic cultures, Berger wrote, "an animal's blood flowed like human blood, but its species was undying and each lion was Lion, each ox was Ox. This was reflected in the treatment of animals. They were subjected *and* worshiped, bred *and* sacrificed." Pre-modern cultures, in other words, were apparently able to see animals as undying spirits dressed, for the moment, in mortal bodies (even if it wasn't clear, at least to me, where the individual spirit of the animal ended and the spirit of the species itself began). That's why the ancient Egyptians, who believed in the reality of the spirit world with a fervency unequaled, arguably, by any other ancient culture, could mummify their beloved pets but *also* mummify other animals simply as tools for sacrifice. They loved and coddled some animals, used others, and—it would seem—didn't fret too much about the difference.

The Animal Soul Today

If the human-animal relationship had generally been a much tougher affair in the past than it was for modern softies like Sarah and me, it occurred to me that the death of an animal— especially a loved animal like an Egyptian queen's favorite cat or one of those Amazonian village monkeys—might in many ways have been a much easier thing to bear back then than it was now. How could such a death not have been an easier thing if something—some mysterious but unquestionably *real* spiritual component—so clearly survived the death of every single animal?

Standing at the grave of my dead rabbit, feeling a sadness that was in no way abstract or theoretical but all too real, I found myself silently asking all kinds of questions that I'd never thought to ask before. If taking a spiritual view of animals had been common practice in ages past, was it possible to take such a view today? Not vaguely or abstractly, but for real? If most people, for most of human history, had been ready to see animals as sacred beings—citizens of a larger country of spirit that their souls returned to when their bodies died—was it possible for a card-carrying member of the modern world like me to genuinely believe that they did so as well? If, in dying, Angus had truly gone (as Berger might have put it) from "rabbit" to "Rabbit"— if his quirky, unquestionably real little personality had not simply disappeared from existence, but had taken on some other, more spiritual form—might it be possible for me to learn more about what that form really was?

Kindred Spirits

A few days after Angus's death, Greg and I traveled to San Francisco to visit another friend of ours who'd moved out to California around the same time I had. On our first night there we paid a visit to City Lights, the city's most famous bookstore. As we normally did when visiting bookstores, Greg headed for the fiction and poetry sections and I went straight to Mythology and Religion. Once there, I found myself scanning the titles with a curious purposefulness. I was (though I might not have admitted as much to Greg had he asked, or to anyone else either) looking for a book: a book that would help me make sense of the questions that had been building in my head ever since Angus's death.

In the few days since Sarah and I had concluded Angus's impromptu little funeral, we had noticed a strange phenomenon. Walking around the apartment, we kept seeing—or rather *almost* seeing—Angus. It was, I would later learn, an experience that countless pet owners who have recently lost a pet know all about. Walking past an area on the floor where the deceased animal liked to lie or sit, one automatically steps slightly to the side so as not to disturb it. As one does so, one sees—or for a moment *thinks* one sees—the animal, right back where it so often used to be.

Not surprisingly, Sarah and I both drew the same half-humorous conclusion about these sightings. "It's Angus's ghost," Sarah had been the first one to say, and though I had laughed when she did so, a part of me wasn't laughing at all. Like the feeling I'd had of Angus's body taking on that strange universality when I'd looked down at him lying dead in his cage, these odd little shadow glimpses were clues to a genuine mystery.

But was it a mystery that could be solved? That was the real question, and that was why I was scanning the spines of the books in front of me in City Lights with such a strange, almost desperate interest.

I didn't find the book I was looking for in City Lights that

night. Not in Mythology and Religion, and not over in Philosophy, and not—when it finally occurred to me to look there—
in Pets or Nature, either. Do animals have souls? If they do,
what happens to those souls when they die? Are animal and
human souls the same or are they somehow different? Do the
world's spiritual traditions agree or disagree on these questions?
Do they even bother to ask them at all? Rather than fade away
in the weeks after Angus's death, these interrelated questions
kept impinging on me at odd and unexpected moments—just as
those shadow-images of Angus kept popping up at the periphery
of my vision back at our apartment.

As it happened, the circumstances of my life as a struggling
freelance writer made it easy for me to keep on looking for answers to these questions—at least in a casual way. With my
book on Mesoamerica out of the way, I did some work for an
environmental book publisher an hour north of us in Venice
Beach. Then a publisher who I knew in New York called out
of the blue and asked if I would be able to provide the text for a
book she was putting together on the history of the monkey in
art. I said yes, and spent the better part of the following year immersed in art and natural history books hunting for details about
how monkeys had been treated and thought about over the centuries. I always turned to the index of these books at some point
to see if the author had anything to say on the subject of the
animal soul.

The more indexes and bibliographies I looked through, the
clearer it became why I'd found no book on the subject that
night in City Lights. Though there were books out there on just
about every other animal-related subject one could possibly

think of, I simply could not lay my hands on a single book about the animal soul.

Nor, as far as I could see, did animals make much of an appearance in the books that had been written about the *human* soul. The German scholar Erwin Rohde's daunting two-volume work *Psyche: The Cult of Souls & Belief in Immortality Among the Greeks*, for example—the single most celebrated academic book on Greek ideas about the afterlife written in the last century—contained exactly two mentions of animals in its index: one on the proper handling of animals slated for sacrifice to the gods, and the other on the question of whether or not initiates in the Eleusinian mysteries (an enigmatic religious ritual centering around symbolic death and rebirth that flourished for centuries in ancient Greece) were vegetarians. The Greeks may have been the first to ask many of philosophy's most important and enduring questions, but "Do animals have souls?" did not seem to have been at the top of their list.

East Versus West

Not that this lack of entries was all that surprising. Even before my research for the monkey book reinforced it, I had known that when it came to looking at animals in a positive, nonjudgmental light, it was Eastern rather than Western culture that had done the best job.

The all-time champions of Eastern mystical nature appreciation were the Taoists of ancient China. Lao Tzu, the mysterious and semi-mythical author of the *Tao Te Ching*, was said to have loved the untouched natural world so much, and to have cared so little for the ways of civilized humanity, that some 2,500 years ago he climbed atop a water buffalo and vanished into the wilderness, scribbling down the *Tao Te Ching* at the request of a gatekeeper he met on his way into the wild.

Though the *Tao Te Ching* is not a book about nature per se, but a manual of human conduct, not a single one of its eighty-one compressed, poetic, and often highly enigmatic chapters fails to allude to nature in some manner. For Lao Tzu, nature in its pristine state is the most perfect earthly manifestation of the Tao—the mysterious force that gave birth to the universe and invisibly upholds it. To act in a way contrary to the Tao, Lao Tzu felt, destroys the potential for human happiness at its root, for humans are part and parcel of the Tao even when they seem to act against it.

Chuang Tzu, Taoism's second great exponent, placed an even more direct emphasis on nature and its creatures as the perfect exemplars of a life in harmony with the Tao. The most oft-quoted passage from Chuang Tzu's writings describes a dream in which he becomes a butterfly. Awakening, he asks a question that gave birth to volumes of philosophical speculation on the true nature of individual identity: "Did Chuang Tzu dream that he was a butterfly? Or did the butterfly dream that he was Chuang Tzu?"

Like everything Chuang Tzu wrote, this passage is couched so simply that it is easy to overlook the complex thinking that underlies it. As the scholar of Taoism Toshihiko Izutsu writes, Chuang Tzu and the butterfly are "indistinguishable, each having lost his or its essential self-identity. And yet, [Chuang Tzu] says, 'there is undeniably a difference between [him] and a butterfly.' " One of the core insights of Taoism is that while on the surface life seems to be a great and teeming multiplicity, on a level "above" our ordinary experience, difference essentially vanishes. On the phenomenal level of life that each of us wakes up to and struggles through every day, a man cannot be a butterfly, and a butterfly can't be a man. But, says Izutsu, "these two things which are thus definitely different and distinguishable from each other do lose their distinction on a certain level of human consciousness, and go into a state of undifferentiation."

Does that mean that on the spiritual level there is no such thing as separate identity? Yes and no, for in both its simplest and its most complex statements, Taoism resolutely refuses to give any easy answers to the question of what identity actually *is*. (This same refusal was also given by that hybrid offspring of Taoism and Buddhism known as Zen. A famous Zen koan— a question unanswerable in terms of ordinary, discriminative consciousness—asks if a dog possesses the Buddha-nature. The answer to this question is neither yes nor no, but *mu*—an untranslatable word that encompasses and transcends both positive and negative responses.)

Unsatisfactory as this answer is to our everyday, discriminative minds, it is nonetheless the closest thing to a true answer the sages of Taoism and Zen are willing to provide, for at its root all identity, whether human or animal, is of the Tao, and the Tao is beyond definition by mundane, analytical, either-or terms. As Izutsu writes, for Chuang Tzu the Tao "has two different aspects, cosmic and personal. In its cosmic aspect the Absolute is Nature, a vital energy of Being which pervades all and makes them exist, grow, decay, and ultimately brings them back to the original source, while in its personal aspect it is God, the

Creator of Heaven and Earth, the Lord of all things and events. As conceptions and representations, the two are totally different from one another, but in reality both point to exactly one and the same thing. The difference between Nature and God is merely a matter of points of view, or the ways in which the human mind conceives of the Absolute which is in itself wholly unknown and unknowable."

Taoism's refusal to establish any cut-and-dried separation between humankind and the natural world is mirrored in its art, just as it is in the art of Zen and the other great faith traditions of the East. Hinduism's democratic attitude toward the natural world and its creatures is immediately evident to a visitor to any of its temple structures, where carved serpents, monkeys, elephants, and other animals crowd the pillars, walls, and ceilings in such numbers that they sometimes threaten to outnumber the human images present. The two most popular and unambiguously lovable gods in the Hindu pantheon, both in India's temple-building past and today when they preside in plastic form over family kitchens or dangle from taxicab rearview mirrors, are the elephant god Ganesh and the monkey god Hanuman. Both gods stand for human qualities (Hanuman for loyalty, Ganesh for the ability to overcome obstacles), but both are also very definitely understood to be *animals*, not just humans outfitted in animal garb. As such, they demonstrate Hinduism's firm belief that divinity encompasses the animal world every bit as much as it encompasses the world of gods and humans.

At the source of Taoism and Hinduism's universally generous spiritual attitude toward earth's creatures is one essential insight: whether it goes by the name of the Tao or Brahma (the

Hindu term for the supreme reality), this ultimate divine reality is the true hidden identity of every created being. (Or as Alan Watts, the popular British writer on Eastern mysticism, used to like to say, "We're it.") Though humans can be seen as superior to other creatures by nature of their greater capacity for understanding, the individuals who attain to the highest levels of that understanding are unanimous, in these traditions, in their assertion that all creation is alike in being a manifestation of the Godhead. Thus, 2,500 years ago, Lao Tzu could write that "when the intelligent and animal souls are held together in one embrace, they can be kept from separating," and just a little over a hundred years ago the modern Hindu saint Ramakrishna could demonstrate the inherent holiness of all creation by allowing animals to eat from plates of food set out as offerings to the gods.

The Eastern Circle and the Western Arrow

Refreshingly democratic as this attitude sounds to the ears of Westerners who are tired of hearing about how much more important humans are than animals, the faiths of the East, while celebrating animals, also raise a number of important questions about the nature of animal identity. This isn't all that surprising, as these faiths also raise many questions about the nature of *human* identity as well. Sooner or later, all Westerners who have grown disillusioned with their own faiths and seek an alternative to it in the wisdom of the East run up against the Eastern attitude toward individual personality: an attitude that is profoundly different from the one bequeathed to us by the faiths

of the West. My own introduction as a teenager to the Eastern faith traditions came not just in the form of books but from my stepbrother Nicky, a monk in the Gelugpa school of Tibetan Buddhism. Nicky took his vows of monkhood in 1986, a year after my stepmother (and Nicky's mother) Betty died of cancer. In the years leading up to that decision, I had the opportunity to see how his practice of Buddhism contrasted with the other chief source of my early ideas on Eastern spirituality: my father.

As a writer specializing in the occult and the esoteric, my father felt it was his duty to embody an attitude of more than simply scholarly interest in the topics he wrote about. Some of these ideas fit better than others, and none suited my father quite as naturally as the quintessentially Eastern idea of reincarnation. The notion that he had walked the earth in previous days struck my father as exceedingly cheering—just as it did many another convert to alternative spiritualities in the sixties and seventies. Reincarnation, in my father's view, transformed human life in an instant from an empty joke into a grand and glorious piece of theater: a millennia-long spectacle with untold dramas in the past and untold more to come. The question "why are we here?" was, for my father, not only answered by the theory of reincarnation, but answered brilliantly: we are here to learn, and to grow: to move from life to life as children shift from classroom to classroom over the years, moving steadily toward that day when they will graduate from incarnate existence altogether as spirit-beings of unimaginable size and brilliance.

When Nicky became a Buddhist, I at first assumed that he held to the same general beliefs about reincarnation as my father. Humans went in and out of one life after another, growing and

deepening all along the way. That, however, turned out not to be quite the case, for Nicky's view of rebirth—the classic Buddhist one—was that it was not so much a forward-pointing arrow as a circle. For my father and his friends, life in the reincarnational universe was above all else a positive event: an adventure with good parts and bad parts, but one that, in the last analysis, was entirely worth embarking on. But the Buddha—and, to a slightly less drastic degree, most of the sages of the other great Eastern faith traditions as well—took a different view. For them, the last thing in the world any self-respecting discarnate soul would want was to reincarnate—for the simple reason that incarnate existence entailed suffering. Endless, *circular* suffering. From the Eastern perspective, the "wheel of karma" (as both Buddhism and Hinduism call the mechanism of cause and effect that keeps the soul returning to body after body) is not the kind of contraption anyone in his or her right mind would want to linger on. Why should they, when—like all wheels—it doesn't really go anywhere but where it's already been before?

This fact has suggested to some that Eastern religions are somehow "anti-life," but it would be more correct to say that they are neither for nor against life, but very much in favor of its transcendence. Generally speaking, for the faiths of the East it is hard to place any genuinely lasting investment in incarnate existence because the self—that heroic actor who in my father's new-age version of things moved from life to life gathering ever new experiences—*simply doesn't exist* on an ultimate level. For the religions of the East, life, seen truly, is a play without actors— a confused dream that evaporates the moment the reincarnating soul awakens to the fact that its existence as a separately existing being is pure illusion. From the ultimate standpoint, there is only the Tao, or Brahman, or Sunyata (a Buddhist term usually translated as "emptiness" but which really means a state of absolutely nonconceptual oneness that cancels out even the notion of divinity). Recovering the knowledge of Brahma, or the Tao, or the Brahma-less void proclaimed by the Buddha, is the one thing—the *only* thing—that really counts in life. Everything else—from the horrors of human suffering to vacations at the beach, to fame and fortune and wine and women and song, and even all the way up to the highest achievements of art and science and ethics and all the rest of it—are, in comparison to this single, saving insight, just one big fat distraction.

For much of my teenage years and early twenties, I puzzled over the relative merits of my father's life-is-an-adventure view of the cosmos, and Nicky's life-is-a-problem-needing-to-be-solved view of it. Who was right? I was never quite able to decide. But one thing that *did* become clear to me was that there was something at the heart of the Eastern faiths that left me a little hungry. Many people, from the comparative religionist Huston Smith to the Dalai Lama, have suggested that whenever possible, one should start out from one's own faith tradition rather than attempting to put on a new one. The older I got, the more sense this idea made, at least for myself, and though I never lost my interest in Eastern faiths, as the years went on I tried more and more to make sense of what they had to say to me from a Western perspective.

More precisely, a Christian one. Was I, I wondered, in anything more than a nominal way, a Christian? What made me

suspect I was in the end was my inability to let go of the idea
of the singular importance of the *particular*. Just as life, for the
religions of the West, is not a circle that goes round and round
but an arrow going somewhere, so the travelers on that road of
life are singular and definite beings: beings who will not lose the
particularities of their earthly identity when the great journey is,
someday and somehow, finished.

One Day in the Park

My long-standing interest—or perhaps obsession—with the
question of what happens to the particularity of a being when
it dies was, of course, not limited to what happens to human
beings. And it was here—with the question of what the Eastern
faiths have to say about the fate of the *animal* soul at death—
that the old question of reincarnation that Nicky and my father
introduced me to took on a new wrinkle.

In the more recently developed Western occult or esoteric
philosophies dealing with reincarnation (groups like the Theoso-
phists, for example, who are responsible for many of the chief
ideas of the new age), it is all but taken for granted that humans
are humans and animals are animals, and one does not come
back in the form of the other. In the East however, it's just the
opposite. Not only is it possible for a human, as he or she suffers
the endless turnings of phenomenal existence, to be reborn as an
animal, it is overwhelmingly *likely* that he or she will. Reincarnation (or metempsychosis, as it's more properly called when
human *and* animal incarnations are involved) in human form is

a supremely rare and fortunate event. This is because in most Eastern reincarnational philosophies, the only way to get off the wheel of birth and death is via a human incarnation.

When I think of what I've learned from Nicky and my father about Eastern versus Western ideas about the shape and nature of the soul's journey through time and how it relates to animals, my mind always goes back to a spring afternoon not too long after I'd finished my book on the monkey in art, when Nicky and I were sitting in a New York City park, discussing the afterlife—in particular, the afterlife of Betty, Nicky's mother, who by then had been dead from cancer for almost a decade. It was one of the first really warm days of the year, and the park was alive with squirrels. Hopping from tree to tree and loping across the new spring grass, they went about their business with that trademark mix of curiosity and indifference to the people around them that has long made squirrels such unrivaled champions at getting along in our human-dominated world.

"So as a Buddhist," I said to Nicky, "you really and truly believe that Betty could actually be one of these squirrels in front of us, right?"

"Absolutely," said Nicky. "Buddhist teaching says that when we die, we bring the accumulated results of all our actions with us into the afterlife state. All the choices my mother made in her life dictated what she would become in her next incarnation— and that incarnation could take place on any level: earthly, heavenly, or hellish. Animal existence is just one of the worlds she could have come into, but it's certainly a possible one. So yes, she could indeed be one of these squirrels right here."

A particularly young and inexperienced-looking squirrel, no

doubt born earlier that same spring, stopped in front of our
bench, stood up on its hind legs, and moved its head up and
down in that quick, jerky way that squirrels do when sizing up
a situation. I looked at that squirrel and tried to imagine my
stepmother's soul squished down into its compact gray body—
her personality transformed into the alert, engaging, but at the
same time decidedly nonhuman consciousness that sparkled in
its eyes.

"I just don't see how Betty could be in there," I said.

"Why not?" said Nicky.

"It's not because I don't like squirrels. But squirrels are . . .
squirrels. Just like dogs are dogs and hippopotamuses are hippopotamuses. To me, the idea that a human personality could simply be translated into an animal personality just doesn't make
sense."

A woman with a pair of straining Jack Russell terriers walked
by, sending the young squirrel back onto the grass and up a tree.

"It seems most obvious to me that people are different from
animals," I said, "when I see a person with their dog. People
who write about dog behavior say that dogs look at their owners
the same way that wolves look at the dominant member of their
pack. But that doesn't seem right to me. I think people are *more*
to dogs than that. In fact, I think that dogs are actually kind
of grateful to people for being people and *not* dogs. Just as all
animals are. There's just something about humans that makes
us . . . different. Not because we're smarter or can think logi-
cally or use language or tools or any of that stuff that people used
to think separated us from the rest of nature, because it's pretty
much been established that there are animals out there that can

do all of those things, too. Whales talk to each other, chimps use tools, and African gray parrots use logic to solve problems. So it's nothing to do with those things. It's something more mysterious. Something that just sets humans off from everything else in creation. But . . . I guess that's not a very Buddhist idea."

Nicky's reply took me by surprise. "Well," he said, "that's not completely true. Buddhists certainly believe that humans are set apart from all other beings as well. It's only from the human state that one can achieve complete enlightenment. That's why it's so important to make use of the human incarnation when one has been fortunate enough to receive one. And it's also why we have such a deep responsibility toward all other beings. It's why Rinpoche is working so hard these days with Jack Benny."

"Jack Benny?"

Nicky's rinpoche, or Buddhist teacher, was a reincarnated Tibetan llama. And Jack Benny, Nicky explained, was his cat. "Rinpoche found him outside his apartment a few years ago when he was just a kitten," Nicky told me. "He decided to do everything he could to make sure that when Jack Benny came back next time, he would receive a human incarnation."

To accomplish this, Nicky told me, Rinpoche set about saturating Jack Benny with Buddhist teaching. As Jack Benny lounged on Rinpoche's lap, Rinpoche would lay out the details of Buddhist metaphysics to him: how all sentient beings are prey to suffering because of the forces of fear, anger, desire, and ignorance; how the Buddha, meditating beneath the Bodhi tree, achieved complete and unconditional enlightenment by realizing the emptiness of all phenomena; how all beings that are sentient (that is, capable of feelings, and hence of suffering) should strive for a human incarnation so that they, too, can achieve enlightenment and thus attain freedom from the pain of incarnate existence themselves; and how the bodhisattvas (enlightened beings) of the world all refuse to exit from existence into total and perfect enlightenment until they can bring all of creation—each and every living thing in the universe—along with them, too.

When busy with other things or away from his apartment, Rinpoche bombarded Jack Benny with an endless succession of recorded dharma talks by the Dalai Lama. By the time Jack Benny was ready to move on from his current feline body, Rinpoche had every hope that, after a brief stretch of time in the Bardo realm (the spirit world where, according to Buddhist belief, human and animal souls go in between incarnations), the former cat would return in a human body, and so have a chance at achieving enlightenment and permanent release from the pain of birth and death himself.

Nicky and I didn't arrive at any rock-solid agreement that day in the park. He continued to see it as perfectly believable that his mother could return to earth in the body of a squirrel (or a mosquito or a cockroach for that matter), and I continued to find it difficult, if not impossible, to imagine that animals and people could trade souls in such a complete and total way.

But though it yielded nothing in the way of ultimate answers, our talk stuck with me all the same. It seemed to sum up both the main question I had often asked about Eastern religions (What happens to the human *personality?*) and the question I had more recently been trying to answer in my animal-soul searches (What happened to *Angus?*).

Enlightenment for One and All

One image in particular stayed in my mind following my conversation with Nicky: that of the Buddha seated beneath the Bodhi
tree seeking enlightenment not just for himself but for all sentient beings. I'd heard that story about the Buddha many times
before, but for some reason, hearing it that day in the park with
all those squirrels running around, it felt . . . *significant* in a way
it never had before.

As Nicky made clear in his story of Rinpoche and Jack
Benny, the sages of the East (not just those of Buddhism, but
of Hinduism and Taoism as well) have by and large encouraged
a much more democratic attitude in their dealings with the rest
of creation than the religions of the West have. In the East, for
example, there is very little talk about humans exercising dominion over the animals. Instead there is an atmosphere of together-
ness: a feeling that whether we're born as a human or a dog or a
cat or a squirrel or even a centipede or grasshopper, we're all in
the same big boat, so that a man who whips his ox or elephant
in this incarnation can expect to come around next time as an
ox or elephant himself. As Mahatma Gandhi put it, "I want to
realize brotherhood or identity not merely with the beings called
human, but I want to realize identity with all life, even with such
things as crawl upon the earth."

That, of course, is the good part. What I came to see as the more
problematic part of the Eastern attitude toward animals (and it's
hinted at in Gandhi's use of "identity" in the quote above) is the
tendency of the Eastern religions to downplay the significance of
particularity: the fact that not only is each animal species unique

unto itself, but so, too, is each member of that species. Not only
does the "catness" of cats and the "elephantness" of elephants
often get lost in the Eastern picture of animals, but so too does
the sense that not only are dogs very different creatures from
cats, but every dog and cat in the world is a unique personality as
well; a personality that deserves to bring its dogness or catness
along with it into the afterlife, just as humans deserve to bring
along their humanness.

One of the paradoxes of Eastern merit-based reincarnational
systems like Buddhism is that they are at the same time intensely dismissive of individual animal personality and intensely
respectful of it. For Rinpoche to believe that Jack Benny might
one day reincarnate as a human was on one level an insult to
Jack Benny's essential catness: that special quality which made
him Jack Benny and no other cat (or other animal) on the planet.
But at the same time, for Kyongola to believe that Jack Benny
was capable, through good works, of rising up the ladder of creation so that he might one day achieve a human incarnation was
to give him high praise indeed, for it suggested that Jack Benny
possessed moral agency—that is, the ability to choose between
right and wrong.

And yet, complimentary to Jack Benny as attributing moral
agency to him clearly was, this attribution did not tell me anything about what I most wanted to know: what would become
of that all-important component of Jack-Benny-ness when he
left the earthly plane behind? This was, in essence, the question
that had lingered at the back of my mind throughout my years
of watching my stepbrother move deeper and deeper into Buddhism. What was sacrificed when one embraced the doctrine

that all was one, and that *all* individual identity, be it human or otherwise, was in some sense an illusion? To imagine Angus, my alfalfa-eating, foot-thumping, nose-twitching, irreducibly individual rabbit returning, far in the future, as a human being was not so much far-fetched to me as it was simply disappointing. I wanted to know what Angus's metaphysical standing was not as some generic, endlessly reincarnating aggregate of fears and desires, but of Angus as the highly individual rabbit that I had known.

Back to the Beginning

It had been my questions about the Eastern versus the Western view of individuality that had first got me interested in studying the religious beliefs of primitive cultures. If East and West differed so profoundly on the question of individual identity, perhaps the origins of this disagreement, and an answer to the question of who was right, might be found among the earth's primal peoples.

That suspicion had led me to my investigations of the Maya and Aztecs, and it now drew me to look toward the primitives for answers to my questions about the animal soul as well. The more primitive a culture, the more likely it is to be interested in animals. The great European cave paintings of the Paleolithic (otherwise known as the Old Stone Age, that vast period extending from the first evidence of tool use among pre-hominids some 2.5 million years ago to the invention of agriculture around ten thousand years ago) were created over a period of some 20,000 years (from about 32,000 BCE to 10,000 BCE), and are the earliest known examples of "true" art (that is, works whose aesthetic function is on a par with or exceeds their utilitarian function). They are composed almost exclusively of images of bison, horses, mammoths, and other such Ice Age species. The stick-figure humans in these pictures—what few of them there are—tend to show up on the edges, almost as afterthoughts. Animals appear in the myths and legends of all cultures, but it's a basic rule that the older the myth, the more animals will figure in it and the more central those animals will be to whatever's going on in the plot.

Why are animals so important to primitive cultures? One big reason is that for primitives (just as for the sages of the East), animals and people aren't really all that different from each other. This belief caused considerable irritation to the anthropologists, linguists, and other scholars of the late nineteenth and early twentieth centuries who pioneered the serious academic study of primitive philosophical thought. The nineteenth-century anthropologist E. B. Tylor coined the term *animism* to describe the primitive belief that natural objects (not just animals but plants and even things like stones and rivers and stars) possessed living, conscious souls just as people do. (Technically, *animism* describes Tylor's theory, not the practice itself, but most writers these days use the term in both ways.) Tylor very definitely didn't think the perspective he described with his theory was true, and his disdain for the primitive ability to look out at the world and feel the world looking back was widely echoed by his fellow academics. "The child-like mind," one of them remarked, "makes no arbitrary distinctions between intelligence as manifested by man and intelligence as manifested by brutes: where it sees actions implying intelligence, there it believes intelligence exists."

Plants and Birds and Rocks and Things

"Child-like" is the operative term here. All primitive societies, the early scholarly theories ran, were essentially like groups of children who gazed about them and innocently imagined all kinds of human things going on in places where they really weren't. In this view, a Stone Age hunter or modern-day Amazonian tribesman who saw consciousness and personality at work in the creatures (and, even worse, in the trees and rocks) he shared the world with was basically no different from two-year-old Stephen Webb, sitting on the floor of the post office, ascribing all manner of volition, emotion, pathos, and humanity to a soon-to-be-squashed ladybug. Animals might be many things, these scholars argued, but they were *not* human beings in fuzzy suits—and the fact that primitives so consistently wanted to pretend that they were just showed how hopelessly naïve these peoples were in comparison to us more insightful moderns.

Snooty and superior as I found most of these academic dismissals of primitive experience to be, I definitely understood that there was something weird about the degree to which primitive peoples humanized the animals they lived among. After all, primitive peoples saw actual, flesh-and-blood animals every day. They watched them and hunted them, and sometimes were even hunted *by* them. Primitives should have been the first to see what, to any modern viewer, is completely obvious: animals might be fellow soul-beings worthy of respect as such, but they don't act like people at all.

And yet it's clear from all the research done on primitives that unlike us, they really *don't* see animals and humans as different—at least as far as we can tell. The contemporary anthropologists Rosalie and Murray Wax, for example, write that in the tales Native Americans told around the fire, animals "reside in lodges, gather in council, and act according to the norms and regulations of kinship. . . . They visit, smoke, gamble, and dance together; they exchange wisdom; they compete in games and combat; and they even marry and beget offspring." Tales from primitive cultures in other parts of the world are full of the same kind of thing. A tribal people that lived by, say, an African river would have no trouble imagining the crocodiles that lived within its waters going about human activities while underwater and out of sight of humans. Like characters in a Beatrix Potter story, they might hold meetings, get into arguments, and consult their leaders on matters of importance. But unlike a group of modern animators who might make a cartoon of crocodiles going about such activities, the primitives would feel no distance or irony while imagining such scenes—no appreciation for the absurdity of the idea that they could actually happen. From childhood on, we moderns enjoy, every bit as much as primitives do, stories in which animals dress up and act like human beings, but unless we're very young children we don't get confused about the fact that animals *don't really do these things.* When primitives told stories about animals, this crucial difference between reality and fancy seemed to be lost.

The French scholar of primitive thought Lucien Levy-Bruhl commented on all of this long ago in his pioneering book *The Soul of the Primitive.* "From our own childhood," Levy-Bruhl wrote, "our fairy-tales have accustomed us to viewing animals behaving like men, and vice versa. We amuse ourselves by attributing to certain animals our passions and our methods of acting; we make of some of them—such as the fox, bear, lion, etc.—the living symbol of a characteristic and of a vice." Primitive peoples, said Levy-Bruhl, did exactly the same thing. But "to the primitive who also amuses himself with such tales, this gulf [between human and animal] does not exist. In his eyes the transit from animal to man and from man to animal is accomplished in the most natural way, without astonishing or shocking anybody."

Spirits in the Material World

Hidden in that word *transit* is the real answer to why primitives are able to think this way about animals. A transit from one state to another—from animal to human, say—can only be made by a being whose identity isn't totally defined by either of those states. According to the primitive view, the animal we see going about its business down here on earth isn't the real animal at all. Fur, fins, and pointy teeth are nothing more than a disguise or outfit, which the true or essential animal can as easily leave behind as a visitor to a swimming pool can leave behind his or her clothing in the changing room. "It was," the contemporary anthropologist David M. Guss writes in *The Language of the Birds*, "and still is in many places, a widely held belief that the part of the animal we see is not the real part but only a disguise, an outfit it wears when it comes to visit our world. Once home again, it removes that costume and changes back into its true form—a form which in most cases is said to be no different from that of the humans." Frank G. Speck writes that according to the Montagnais-Naskapi Indians of Quebec and Labrador, animals are, in terms of their emotions and their inner sense of identity and purpose in life, just like people. The real difference between man and animals, say the Montagnais-Naskapi, lies in what is outside, not in what's inside. Their myths state that at the beginning of the world, before humans came into existence, animals talked like humans and were largely indistinguishable from them. "When addressing animals in a spiritual way in his songs," writes Speck, "or using the drum, the conjurer uses the expression . . . 'you and I wear the same covering and have the same mind and spiritual strength.' This statement was explained as meaning not that men had fur, not that animals wore garments, but that their equality was spiritual and embraced or eclipsed the physical." The scholar of Native American thought John Bierhorst writes that among the Tlingit of southeast Alaska, "animal souls are called *qwani*, 'inhabitants of,' because they are believed to live inside the animal's fleshly body. Since the same word is used for the inhabitants of a house or a village, the alternate translation 'people' is permissible. One speaks of *xat qwani*, 'fish people.' "

When we in the modern world look at a person or an animal we see a living being trapped in, and defined by, the complex, doomed machinery of a body made of muscle and tendon, blood and bone. Primitive humanity saw the same thing. But they also saw, behind the person or animal in its physical form, another, larger form that we in the modern world *don't* see, or at least don't see nearly as clearly: a soul or spirit that navigated the painful and problematic theater of material existence for a time, but which did not come to an end when the physical body died. "The creature's body," writes Bierhorst, "is always a separate quantity. For example, a Tlingit may say that the body of the killer whale is the canoe for the killer whale *qwani.* The more widespread idea, however, is that the body is merely a disguise, perhaps a cloak or a mask." In the primitive view, the true or essential animal is a *spiritual entity,* and all its external bodily trappings are just that: *external* and nothing more.

Is all this anthropomorphic? Not really. To anthropomorphize is to look at an animal and see a human being in a furry suit (the way Greg felt Sarah and I did in our more indulgent moments with Angus). But that, according to Guss, Bierhorst, and others, isn't actually what primitives do. When an African tribesman or an Australian Aborigine or an Indian from the Brazilian rain forest looked at an anteater or a kangaroo or a giant otter, what they were really seeing in each case was a being in a suit all right, but it was a *spiritual* being—one whose true identity was connected to, but not ultimately defined by, the earthly outfit it was wearing. Just as, when they looked around their village, they would see other spirits in the guise of men, women, and children. If a single line were needed to define the primitive view of existence, it might be borrowed from a song by The Police that always gives me pause when I hear it: "We are spirits in the material world."

The Primitives Versus the Far East

When that hypothetical anteater or kangaroo or otter mentioned above died, its spirit returned to join the rest of its kind in a place where the distinctions that so clearly separated humans and animals in the material world *still existed, but to a lesser degree than they did on earth.* For, make no mistake about it, among the great majority of primitive peoples, when an animal died and its soul left its body, it continued to hold on to its identity as a member of that specific species and no other. Many primitive myths and legends tell us that when animals leave the earth behind, they turn into people. But, as Bierhorst pointed out, this is not the same as saying that in doing so they become *identical* to human beings; rather, they simply become more humanlike, so that on the spiritual level personhood becomes a quality that all creation shares.

To help explain this knotty issue, Bierhorst points to an essay by the anthropologist A. Irving Hallowell, who in the 1930s worked with the Ojibwa people around Lake Winnipeg. Hallowell, says Bierhorst, "concluded that animals, plants, and objects were indeed persons—except that here, 'person' is not the same as 'human.' Rather, it is a larger, more inclusive category." In other words a "person" in the Ojibwa universe isn't actually a human being at all; it's something bigger than that. And it's spiritual, not physical, in nature.

All people, all animals—and even, in many mystical conceptions, all objects—are never truly and wholly "themselves" while on earth, for it is only in the world above this one that every created thing, even a rock or a leaf of grass, recovers its true identity. While the physical body is useful and necessary for navigating the physical world, it is also a rather terrible encumbrance. Not only are we more limited in movement while in our bodies than we are as spirits; we are also, to a greater or lesser degree, limited mentally—that is, in terms of our knowledge of who and what we really are. When a whale or a salmon or a bear or a giraffe dies, according to the primitive view, each of those creatures recovers the spiritual identity that it in part was forced to forget in the descent to the physical plane. When it dies and returns to that higher level of existence, the animal enters a world where the attributes used to distinguish it (from size to fur color to general temperament) do not vanish, but where they are subsumed by its more important *spiritual* identity. Just as the physical world is characterized by separation and difference, so the spiritual world is characterized by unity. People and animals there all "live under one roof," as the Nuer people put it. *All beings are first and foremost spirits* in the primitive view, just as they are in the Eastern one. But on the metaphysical level—the level of spirit—there is, for the primitive, not nearly the emphasis on all-transcendent oneness that there is in the East. And the result is that we find in the primitive worldview a spiritual world where difference—between species and between individuals— is upheld rather than abandoned.

The Earth Above the Earth

This mysterious spiritual homeland where the souls of humans and animals go when they die, and where they appear in their original, luminous, more-than-earthly form, has been described in the myths and legends of primitive (and not so primitive) peoples from all around the world since the dawn of time. The story of the drop out of "our first world" (as T. S. Eliot called this place of original innocence in his poem "Burnt Norton") into the present world of work, sex, hunger, and general discord is, in fact, probably the single oldest and most universal story there is. Polynesians, Arctic Eskimos, and African Pygmies are all in agreement that our fall out of that world involved, first and foremost, a transition from a state where people and animals lived in happy, spiritualized coexistence into a world defined by what could be called *parasitism*: the preying of one group of bodily creatures upon another for the purpose of survival. This is the transition that the Nuer myth summed up so neatly with the words "stomach entered into man." Long ago and far away, something somehow went wrong: a mistake or accident or infraction on the part of man or beast or both brought all creatures out of alignment with the Source that gave them birth. The material world as we know it today arose as a result of this primal falling-away, and within it all animals and all humans, no matter how well intentioned, are forced to prey upon one another—to make use of the sustenance provided by one another's bodies in order to live. But this fact, troublesome as it is, does not (or at least should not) remove the memory of that higher, more spiritual world from which both humans and animals descended. Looked at with the right eyes (that is, eyes that see past the seeming completeness of the physical dimension), both humans and animals remain in essence what they have always been: spirits living in the physical world.

If any of this sounds vaguely biblical, that's because the story of Adam and Eve's fall out of a state of original spiritual perfection into a world of strife and discord is simply the Hebrew version of this same universal story. If it sounds a little Platonic, it's because Plato's vision of a world of perfect Forms existing above and beyond the limitations and shortcomings of the material world is also, in essence, a retelling of the same story as well—this time in philosophical rather than mythical guise.

According to most versions of the fall-from-paradise story, just because the earthly and spiritual worlds are no longer one does not mean that the spiritual world where humans and animals originally dwelt together under one roof has disappeared completely. On the contrary, it has only retreated to a place above earth: a place close enough that it is still (at least for some individuals on some occasions) within reach.

The Primordial Geography

For many primitive peoples, the universe was divided into three levels stacked like pancakes one on top of the other. The middle level was the visible world—the place where daily life unfolded. Just above it lay the heavenly region where the souls of humans and animals returned after their travails in the middle region were done. Below the ground, meanwhile, lay a realm where other kinds of spirits lived—some but not all of them frightening and sinister. When a person died, his or her soul might descend to the land beneath the earth for a time, but more often than not it would end up, perhaps after a trial or two, in the heavenly region above the earth (much as Dante, journeying through hell and purgatory in *The Divine Comedy*, finally ends up in paradise).

Though separate, these three worlds were usually joined at one point—often by a sacred mountain or a great tree that rose up at their very center like a spindle piercing a stack of three LP records. It was by means of this magical tree or mountain that the shaman or medicine man—the primitive spiritual practitioner in charge of maintaining humanity's relationship to the divine—typically traveled when he journeyed to the worlds above and below in spirit form. When a person grew ill and the spirits of death or disease pulled his or her soul down into the lands beneath the earth, it was the shaman's job to travel down and retrieve it. Likewise when a person died and his or her soul journeyed to the spirit world above the earth to stay, it was the shaman's job to make sure the soul found its way there without getting lost in the underworld, and that it felt thoroughly at home in the heavenly region once it had arrived.

With all kinds of minor variations, this was the basic primordial model of the universe, and every spiritual view of the world that has come along since owes something to it. Here's how Richard Heinberg, author of *Memories and Visions of Paradise*, describes the architecture of earth and heaven—the top two records in that stack of three—as it has appeared in countless mythologies across the face of the earth:

> According to universal tradition, the original earthly Paradise and the still-existent otherworldly Paradise were at first united, or in any case were in close proximity and communication. The means of connection is described variously in

different cultures—most vividly, perhaps, as a rainbow. In the traditions of Japan, Australia, and Mesopotamia, the rainbow was seen as a reminder of a bridge that once existed between Heaven and Earth and was accessible to all people. The seven colors of the rainbow were the seven heavens of Hindu, Mesopotamian, and Judaic religion. Among the central Asians, shamanic drums were decorated with rainbows symbolizing the shaman's journey to the Otherworld. Similarly, the seven levels of the Babylonian ziggurat (stepped pyramid) were painted with the seven colors of the rainbow, and the priest, in climbing its stories, symbolically mounted to the cosmic world of the gods.

Within this old spiritual geography, the shaman was the primary guide, for it was the shaman alone who possessed the ability to travel beyond the earthly plane without getting lost or injured. The shaman in turn relied for his information on the spirits of land, lake, and sea. But he also relied on animals: not just animals in spirit form, but the actual, flesh-and-blood ones with whom he shared his world. The medicine men and women whose job it was to keep earthly humanity in touch with its original spiritual homeland knew that if you wanted to know what was going on up in heaven, you watched the animals down here on earth.

Wisdom Through Friendship

Why, if animals are fallen just as we are, did the primitive spiritual practitioner look to them for knowledge of the world beyond? The short answer is that animals haven't fallen quite so far or hard as we have.

The evidence for this belief is everywhere in primitive thought. If earth is a place of doubt and indecision, heaven is a place of certainty and assurance, and it is animals, not humans, who know and remember this best. Unlike humans, who are always questioning and second-guessing themselves, animals are rarely at a loss for what to do—and for the primitives the reason for this was obvious: animals were simply in closer touch with that original spiritual landscape above the earth than humans are.

We in the modern world are just as aware as our primitive forebears were that animals usually know how to proceed with their lives with much less fuss than we do. But we have become so accustomed to chalking this fact up to "instinct" that we have lost our appreciation for just how mysterious this built-in knowledge really is. This wasn't the case with early humanity. For them, the fact that a goose or a caribou or a salmon could return every year to the same place to feed or mate, the fact that certain grazing animals knew exactly when certain plants were going to come into bloom or when the weather was going to turn warm or cool, indicated an essential difference between all animals and humans. Though humans were the masters of what we call *culture* (all those countless innovations, from bows and arrows to clothing to houses to written language, that each tribe learned and passed down from generation to generation), animals were the masters of the realm from which all these gifts had first originated. Thus, in the Nuer myth, it is from animals that humans are said to have first learned the arts of culture, even though down here on earth it is humans, and humans alone, who practice them.

All of which goes to show why the shamans or medicine men that were early humanity's spiritual leaders always had animals for teachers. During his initiation, Mircea Eliade writes, "the shaman is supposed to meet with an animal who reveals to him certain secrets of the craft, or teaches him the *language of the animals*, or who becomes his *familiar spirit*." To engage spiritually with an animal was to link oneself not to a lower level of creation, but a higher one. "We should note at once," Eliade writes, "that to win the friendship and spontaneous mastery of the animals does not signify, within the horizons of an archaic mind, any regression to a lower biological level. For, on the one hand, animals are charged with a symbolism and a mythology of great importance for the religious life; so that to communicate with animals, to speak their language and become their friend and master is to appropriate a spiritual life much richer than the merely human life of ordinary mortals."

Far from becoming *less* human by associating with animals, it was instead only by virtue of an alliance with them that the earth's first spiritual practitioners could become fully human to begin with. For to be human was to practice the arts of culture, and all those arts were only received and mastered in the wake of the departure from the first world. Animals, because they still lived more within the range of that first world than humans did, were not in need of culture to the degree that humans were. They lived and moved, to an extent, as if they were still *within* that paradise world. And it was because of this that primitive humanity, and the shaman especially, came to watch animals as closely as they did, envying the certainty with which they walked and swam and flew across the earth, and seeking to emulate that surety of movement whenever they could. Though the earth wasn't home—not completely, anyway—animals were clearly at home upon it, and in the things they did and the ways they did them, early humanity found an endless source of inspiration for how they themselves should live and act within the post-paradise world of human work and culture.

The Animal Code of Conduct

Just as it was understood that animals and humans, while different from each other in important ways, shared a kinship through their mutual descent from the First World of spirit, so there were certain basic do's and don'ts that humans needed to observe in their interactions with animals while down on the physical plain. The great majority of the rites and rituals of primitive societies—both those we intuitively understand and those that seem completely incomprehensible and even abhorrent to us—are all designed to address in one way or another the basic intuition that both people and animals are spirits living momentarily in a world of flesh and blood and bone: a dog-eat-dog world where, in order to keep existing, one creature must seek out and prey upon another.

For most of human history (and more especially prehistory) the principal form this preying-upon other creatures took was, of course, hunting. As Mircea Eliade put it, humankind itself is essentially the result of a single decision made at the dawn of time: "the decision to kill in order to live." (Or, as the nature writer

Paul Shepard memorably put it, "mind would be the child of the hunt.") Our hominid ancestors only rose above their pre-hominid fellows by becoming meat eaters, and for more than two million years, as Eliade writes, the "fruits, roots, mollusks, and so on, gathered by women and children, did not suffice to insure the survival of the species." Stated simply, it was killing that made us who and what we are.

Homo sapiens is, as everyone knows, a very young species. Though humanlike creatures have been on earth for some five million years, around two and a half million years ago our hominid ancestors experienced a drastic enlargement in brain size that could only have been fueled by a shift in diet: less roots and berries, more meat.

Not that our ancestors took up weapons and set out to hunt the animals around them overnight. For most of the millennia during which our ancestors acquired their taste for animal flesh, they had to scavenge it as they could, and spent most of their time trying to stay out of the way of other, far more efficient predatory animals interested in consuming *them*. As the archaeologist Steven Mithen puts it, "the earliest members of our genus were not great hunters of wild beasts, but largely sneaky scavengers, creeping in after the lions, hyenas and vultures had had their fill."

For hundreds of thousands of years, early humans survived by a mix of hunting and scavenging, only gradually placing the hunt at the center of their existence. By the time of *Homo sapiens'* older, more heavyset cousin *Homo neanderthalensis* (Neanderthal man), who lived from about 130,000 years ago all the way up to about 27,000 BCE, hunting was most likely an important component of human existence—but it was still very definitely hunting-for-beginners. Neanderthals used simple, stone-tipped spears, and when genuinely out to hunt for meat rather than scavenging it, seem to have practiced a straightforward, no-frills style of hunting that archaeologists call the "confrontation technique"—which, as it sounds, amounted to getting in front of an animal and trying, with little fanfare, to kill it before it bit, trampled, or otherwise did in the hunter.

Only Connect

Though they had larger brains than ours, the Neanderthals do not seem to have been able to use those brains to the same inspired effect that we do. "At present," writes Mithen, "it appears that for several hundred thousand years Neanderthals relied upon a hunting technology of limited effectiveness. It also appears that Neanderthals did not develop any relationships with animals beyond those of predator/prey as had characterized human ancestors for the previous million years. There are no pictorial depictions of animals, no evidence that animals were used as symbols of power and authority, no trace of totemic thinking."

The key term here is *relationship*. Though they possessed those impressively sized brains, Neanderthals remained, in essence, little more than very clever animals. They killed their fellow animals and were killed by them, but they did so without any kind of spiritual technology that would allow them to place the act of killing within a larger background of meaning. There is little evidence that Neanderthals possessed much in the way of art or religion, and the great cave paintings of the Paleolithic that we associate with stone-age humanity were the products of fully modern men and women. They had no equivalents in the Neanderthal world.

Mithen advances the widely accepted opinion that the reason for this lack of fully human sensitivity and imagination on the part of the Neanderthals was due not so much to an absence of knowledge as to a separation of that knowledge into several distinct fields. Neanderthals, he suggests, were clearly intelligent, but that intelligence was compartmentalized into several self-contained areas. Their lack of a sophisticated hunting technology, he writes, "may have been because the detailed and extensive knowledge about animal behavior that they possessed was unable to be integrated with their knowledge about making artifacts so that hunting weapons suitable for killing specific types of animals in specific circumstances could not be designed."

All this changed with the arrival of modern humans, a mere 100,000 years ago. True hunting can be said only to have emerged with humans who were capable of seeing the act within a sacred context: one supported by art, ritual, and religion, and inspired by the ability to consciously experience and appreciate animals as fellow spiritual beings that were both like humans and subtly different from them as well. When humankind became hunters in this sense, they stepped outside of the gates of the natural community—just far enough out that they were able to turn, look back, and see the natural world for what it truly was: a beautiful but also terrible place, characterized by separation rather than unity, and strife rather than accord.

With this change, human beings became unique inhabitants

of earth. Not because they killed (after all, countless other living beings caught up in the problematic realm of material existence did that), but because they *knew* they killed, and because they sought to make spiritual sense of, and spiritual peace with, this fact.

The Birth of Thought

To sum all this up: we are what we are today thanks to animals. This can be said not only because prey animals allowed early hominids to make the jump to genuine *Homo sapiens* status by providing the food that fueled our pre-hominid ancestors' massive increase in brain size, but for another reason that's just as important: *animals taught us how to think.* We humans prize our ability for abstract thought—so much so that until recently we have been very stingy about admitting that any other animal, even the most intelligent, possesses any of the stuff at all. The *New Oxford American Dictionary* definition of *abstract* is "existing in thought or as an idea but not having a physical or concrete existence." If we consider the situation of our ancestors, loitering about at the edges of the predator-prey world, trying to figure out how to get a toe in the door as a genuine predator rather than as a mere scavenger, it is fairly easy to see that one of the first uses of proto-abstractive thinking on the part of those ancestors must have involved learning *to think like other animals.* To be capable of abstraction means, first and foremost, being able to climb out of one's skin—to transcend the barrier of the body through the medium of mind. And it was precisely the early hunters' ability to enter mentally into the skins of the animals around him—thinking their thoughts, feeling their moods, their fears, and their urges—that allowed those hunters to be able to stalk and kill those animals in the more sophisticated, fully human manner that so differentiated *Homo sapiens* from his ancestors.

This early breed of thought was not at all cold or clinical, however. The more you think like another being, the more you identify with it. And the more you identify with it, the more you come to love and admire it. And the more you love and admire it, the more you seek to *be* like it. You draw pictures of it, make paintings of it—even dress up and act like it. And if, along with all this admiration and imitation, you also regularly kill it to stay alive, you have the ingredients for the immeasurably profound, paradoxical, dangerous, and spiritually nourishing relationship that the earth's first hunters had with their prey animals. It was a relationship that, most likely, gave birth not only to human thought, but to the first truly human conception of the sacred as well.

Because primitive humanity understood that killing was the signature act of material existence, no other single act received more attention in the struggle to make spiritual sense of life on earth. Hunting was, in the words of Native American scholar Calvin Martin, a "holy occupation." Most primitive cultures spent at least as much time thinking about spiritual power as they did about the material kind, and this is reflected in the fact that so many different cultures have a specific term for this power. One of the best known, from the Algonkian Indians of Eastern Canada, is *Manitou.* As Martin writes, Manitou is "the force which made everything in Nature alive and responsive to man. Only a fool would confront life without it, since it was only through the manipulation and interpretation of Manitou that man was able to survive in this world. Without Manitou Nature would lose its meaning and potency, and man's activities would become secular and mechanical."

All animals possessed Manitou or sacred power to one degree or another, but large predators and game animals possessed it in spades. When an early group of hunters assembled to kill, let's say, a bison, they knew that there were two basic ways of going about it. They could simply kill the animal and make use of its body—in effect booting its spirit out as a landlord would a tenant whose rent is late—or they could separate spirit from body in such a way that the "true form" of the bison (which, it went without saying, did not die when its body did) would not employ its very considerable sacred power against its killers once it was back in the spirit world.

With the leap in associative thinking that signaled the rise of true *Homo sapiens,* hunting almost instantly became a far more complex activity than it had been for the thousands upon thousands of years when our ancestors were basically just crafty, tool-using apes. Simple spears gave way to slings, bows and arrows, and other, more-sophisticated weapons. The kill-it-quickly-before-it-kills-you method of the Neanderthal confrontationalists was replaced by more-elaborate and sophisticated methods of hunting, in which large and terrifying animals like mammoth and bison were brought down through teamwork, strategic planning, and a knowledge of animal behavior so intense that the hunters became, in an imaginative sense, those animals themselves. Animals could be lured or frightened into compromising areas where they either could not defend themselves from the spears of their hunters, or were herded over cliffs to their deaths, gravity accomplishing what human muscle alone could not. The habits of animals—their likes and dislikes, their migration and breeding habits—were analyzed and exploited by brains that no longer kept information in separate compartments, like the food on a schoolchild's lunch tray, but that allowed those formerly separate compartments to communicate with each other. As a result, knowledge of how an animal lived could be used in order to figure out how to most effectively bring that life to an end.

And along with all this new mental and physical technology for killing came an equally inspired spiritual technology designed to prevent the spirit of the animal killed from being angry for what humans had done to it. Spiritually speaking, no animal killed by human hands ever died alone in the primitive world. Not only was the act of killing tied up with all manner of rules and proscriptions, but the creature's journey back to the spirit realm was monitored (thought about, prayed about, sung about) as well. Sometimes a tribe's shaman would even accompany the soul of the slain animal on its journey—though generally it was assumed that just as animals knew their way around on earth better than humans did, so too were they in little need of direction when it came time to make their way back to the land of spirit. (That sentiment survived, thousands of years later, in the Egyptian belief that the deceased human soul was led to the lands of the dead by his or her dog.)

Spirits of the Species

What was waiting for the animal soul when its body had been appropriated and it returned to the earth-above-the-earth? To answer that question, we need to go back to Berger's statement that for primitives "every lion was really Lion, every ox really Ox." Like instinct, the fact that animals come in different species is something most of us take for granted—at least after we pass out of the initial *dog-cat-horse-cow* excitements of early childhood. But for primitive humanity the fact that animals are different—that each comes with its own markings, its own territories, its own ways of feeding and mating and living and dying—never stopped being intensely interesting. Every child knows that each species of animal not only looks and acts differently, but that it also has a very definite—if hard to define—spiritual feeling or *atmosphere* to it. (A fact that I, along with many another twelve-year-old boy, discovered back in the mid-seventies when *Jaws* brought the near-mystical fascination of sharks to our attention. Meanwhile, it seemed, the girls in my class got this same mysterious feeling about horses.) This feeling of the essential horseness of a horse or the sharkness of a shark is what Plato would later develop into his philosophical theory of Forms, which states that all horses are in fact imitations of an ideal horse that exists in a dimension beyond the physical. Like so many of Plato's ideas, this one dates back, in its pre-philosophical form, to the days of the Paleolithic cave painters: artists who not only felt the horseness of horses and the deerness of deer, but who transferred that feeling to the figures they painted on their cave walls with an elemental sureness of touch that few artists since have managed to equal.

Primitives saw animals in something like the way we see sports teams. Each species of animal not only had its own uniform (the stripes or spots or horns it sported while down here on earth) but its own coach as well: a guardian spirit that was in charge of directing all the individual members of that species while they were alive, and welcoming them back to the spirit world at the time of their deaths. It was in large part because of this guardian spirit that animals were so uncannily sure of how to act. How is a mother sea turtle that is ready to lay her eggs able to find, out of thousands of miles of coastline, the exact beach where she herself was hatched? How does a beaver know how to build a dam, or a swallow how to build a nest in the eave of a barn? "Instinct," we answer once again, confidently yet vaguely. Once again, the primitive answered differently. For the world's first peoples, the everywhere-apparent fact that animals just simply *knew* things that no one on earth had taught them was the result not just of their still-retained connection to heaven, but more specifically of their contact with the various species spirits, each one of which whispered in the ear of every single ox or caribou or wildebeest under its charge: telling it what to do, making sure it didn't ever get lost or confused, keeping it ever in touch with the invisible world above.

But the chain of command did not end with the species spirits—the head caribou, bison, wildebeest, and lion that watched the earthly adventures of the animals in their charge like mothers on the edge of a playground. Beyond those species spirits stood yet another figure: one even more ancient and mysterious.

The Master of Animals

When I was a kid there was a figure that often appeared in my imagination: a being with the body of a man and the physical characteristics of various kinds of animals: a wolf's tail, a lion's claws, the horns of a bull, or the antlers of a deer. Familiar and likable, yet at the same time remote and profoundly mysterious, this animal-man never held completely still in my imagination but changed his features a little every time I pictured him. Sometimes he had a leopard's tail instead of a wolf's, or a horse's hooves instead of claws. At other times he would (briefly) abandon all his human characteristics and become an animal pure and simple. But whatever superficial form he took, and at whatever level of the scale between human and animal he chose to manifest, this animal-man was always, I somehow knew, the *same* being. And the place he came from—a place of wildness, mystery, and pure animal strangeness—always stayed the same as well.

Though my version of this being was my own unique invention, it soon became apparent that other people knew about him, too. Certain stories—in books, comics, or movies—brought this animal-man particularly to mind. While I didn't read many superhero comics myself, I understood that the superheroes held so dear by my friends—Batman, Spider-Man, the X-Men's Wolverine—had more than a trace of this character about them. I was a big fan of monster movies, and in certain of these, like *King Kong*, *The Wolf Man*, or *The Creature from the Black Lagoon*, where the monster turned out to be not so monstrous after all but only mistakenly reviled and misunderstood, it was really always this same figure that I was secretly watching.

The same went for certain kinds of more-realistic stories: those, for example, in which a young boy or girl would befriend some large, dangerous animal only to be told by parents, townsfolk, or some other voice of authority that the animal was a menace and not to be fraternized with. Inevitably the beleaguered animal would end up being pursued and harassed by the representatives of the ordinary world (the police, the government, an angry group of villagers). When this happened, only the young hero or heroine would understand what was really going on: that this creature from beyond the borders of the ordinary world was not the villain of the story at all, but its hero. If (as often happened) the creature died at the end of the story, it did so, I knew, not because it really deserved to, but because the realm it came from—a place much older, deeper, and better than the one I lived in could ever dream of being—was simply more than the ordinary world could handle.

Though this animal-man prowled around at the back of my imagination for years, it wasn't until I started looking into primitive cultures in my twenties that I realized just how independent of my imagination, how completely universal, a figure he really was. As it turned out, he existed just about everywhere in the primitive world. Changing his features as he moved from the deserts of northwestern Australia to the jungles of New Guinea to the plains of the American West, beneath all these variations he remained, in the various paintings, drawings, or grainy photos of primitive tribal rituals I found him in, ever the same.

So who was he?

If, in the basic primitive vision of the cosmos, all animals were spiritual beings clothed in physical bodies, and if the species spirits in the world above were in charge of each individual animal that lived and died down here on earth, those species spirits also had a master of their own. Though he was known by a thousand different names across the span of the primitive world, scholars today call him by the general name of the Lord or Master of Animals. If the shaman is the original model for all of those characters in popular stories (from Jack, the cosmic tree-climbing hero of "Jack and the Beanstalk" all the way down to Harry Potter) who travel from this world to the one beyond, the Master of Animals is the prototype for the wise figure that this traveler inevitably meets with when he gets there. When young King Arthur meets Merlin the magician in *The Sword in the Stone*, or when Luke Skywalker meets the eccentric hermit Obi-Wan Kenobi in the original *Star Wars*, both meetings echo an older meeting that took place in locations past counting in the primitive world. This was an encounter in which a member of the primitive tribe—a member with a certain facility for communing with animals and the spirit world—left the tribe behind to meet with a wise and all-powerful figure who was in charge both of all the species spirits and of the individual animals that those species spirits in turn directed. Would certain of those individual animals consent to being killed and eaten? The Master of Animals was the one who gave the final answer to this question, and on that answer the tribe's life depended.

The Original God-Man

The Master of Animals is the oldest, most consistently identifiable spiritual or supernatural figure in human history—much older than the distinctions between East and West we use to couch so much of our discussions of religion today. The Harappan civilization, for example, which flourished in the Indus Valley of the Indian subcontinent some seven thousand years ago, produced a number of clay seals with a human figure at their center. The Carmelite monk and student of Indian religion Thomas Matus writes that this figure is "seated in a typically yogic posture: the legs are bent so that the soles of the feet touch one another . . . the arms are extended, and the hands rest on the knees. The figure is adorned with bracelets, breastplate, and a horned headdress."

This figure is also, in many cases, surrounded by animals. "Although scholars differ in their reading of the symbolism in these seals," writes Matus, "it seems probable that the image represents that aboriginal deity later called Rudra or Shiva, the Lord of yogis and wild beasts."

The Master of Animals is also present in ancient Greece, where as Orpheus he took up his magical lyre to charm the wild beasts until he was destroyed by forces jealous of his skills. He is present as well in every Far Eastern image of the Buddha or a bodhisattva meditating in the forest with birds, squirrels, and other wild creatures gathered around, and in the images of the great Irish saints and ascetics who lived for so long in the woods that, we are told, birds came to make nests on their heads and in the hair of their beards.

Perhaps most surprisingly, he is present in the New Testament. When the Gospel of Mark tells us, cryptically, that Jesus was "with the wild beasts" during his forty days in the wilderness, a memory of the Master of Animals stands in the background of this statement. He is also there when we are told that God the

Father gave his only begotten son to suffer and die here on earth for the good of humankind. And he is in evidence as well in the notion that once he was dead, this man-god returned to the side of his father in heaven while those below would remember him in a meal in which his flesh and blood were ritually consumed, and through which he would become mystically present to them. This story of a god sympathetic to the forces of both spirit and nature, a god who dies and yet dies not, began in the furthest reaches of prehistory and originally featured an animal rather than a human hero. In the first, immeasurably ancient, versions of this story, the Master of Animals was a god of animals and hunters both: one who allowed an animal to die at the hands of humans and be eaten by them, provided that those humans atoned for their act by venerating the spirit of the animal—and the Master who sent it—once the animal was gone.

The Master of Animals was a being of two worlds, a creature that *changed.* More human than animal, yet always with some animal features, he was, when he took animal form, more likely to appear as certain species than others. Bulls—graceful yet powerful, beautiful yet frightening—dominate the art of the Paleolithic caves, and it's even possible that the word *god* itself traces back, originally, to the pre-Dravidian Indian root *gut,* or "bull." He was also very often—wholly or in part—depicted as a bear. This makes sense as bears—specifically cave bears, a now-extinct species that grew larger than today's grizzly—were a source of considerable terror and fascination for Stone Age humanity. Cave-bear skulls and bones, carefully arranged and either buried in the ground or wedged into crevices in cave walls, are among the earliest pieces of evidence for prehistoric religious activity yet discovered. Bear cults existed all over the northern hemisphere and inspired religious rituals in which a bear is sacrificed and its soul is sent back to heaven as an emissary of the human community (and which often include a "last supper" in which the partial carcass of the bear is present at a feast in its honor). That God took the form of a bear when he created the world is suggested by the Siberian belief that mother bears give birth to their cubs as unformed lumps. Slowly and patiently, it is said, the mothers literally lick these amorphous little blobs into the shape of bears, just as God himself did when he created the ordered world we know today from the primal chaos.

If we live in a sundered world, a world where heaven and earth have fallen into a state of tragic alienation, the Master of Animals is the one figure that can right this situation. He is the living bridge between the two worlds of matter and spirit—the sole figure on heaven or on earth that can make those two regions one once again. And he can do this precisely because he exists neither completely in the world of humans or in the world of animals, but in the space between them: the space that first appeared in the Fall, when human consciousness parted ways with animal consciousness. Through that dual identity, he kept the two worlds one.

Some readers may, at this point, be starting to feel a certain number of reservations: God as an animal-like figure with a tail and horns? Am I not, perhaps, confusing God with someone else? But that, of course, is precisely the point. Before God and the Devil divided themselves up into two separate beings, there was only this single, most ancient of religious figures—this animal-man who was neither completely man nor completely animal, yet somehow more than either.

The Master of Animals is *so* old a figure that he transcends not just the traditional antithesis between the divine and the demonic, but between male and female as well. In many parts of the world there was not only a Master but also a Mistress of Animals—a being that we see echoed in the Greek goddess Artemis, the Roman Diana, and even in contemporary popular images of Mother Nature. The Master and the Mistress of Animals share a large number of features, and it seems very likely that originally the Master of Animals was neither male nor female, but both at once. Before God and the Devil separated, before all the long battles and arguments over matriarchies and patriarchies, before Krishna or Moses or Jesus or Muhammad, there was this sole, singular, and immeasurably consequential figure: a supernatural, animal-like human surrounded by, and at peace with, the human and nonhuman worlds.

The Master in the Modern Age

The rules of order that the Master of Animals enforced in the days of his command had a wide-ranging—and profoundly positive—effect. As the Dutch historian of religion Jan N. Bremmer writes, "as long as the hunting tribes kept their faith in the protector," that is, the Master of Animals, "they were careful to avoid over-killing the game, since they believed they would incur the wrath of the god if they did not."

Provided the rules he instated were adhered to, the Master of

Animals could be very accommodating to humans. "The lord of the animals," writes the historian of religion Otto Zerries, "is often a helper of mankind. He guides the animals to the hunter or helps him discover the trail of his prey. In addition, he often provides a magical weapon or a mystical spell that assures success in finding game. Such assistance, however, often assumes that certain conditions are fulfilled or specific regulations observed: the lord of the animals punishes the malicious, those who wantonly kill more game than is needed and those who are disrespectful of the dead game, especially in handling the bones."

Bones—both animal and human—were of paramount importance to primitive humanity because, like blood, they contained a certain amount of soul power even after the animal that had owned them on earth had moved on again to the spirit world. "The 'soul,' " writes Mircea Eliade, "is presumed to reside in the bones and hence the resurrection of the individual from its bones can be expected."

Resurrection? This concept too, it turns out, was born in the Stone Age. When, in the Book of Ezekiel, the prophet looks out on the valley of dry bones and asks "Lord, can these bones live?" he is asking one of the oldest spiritual questions ever put. It was a question addressed by the earth's first hunters both to an animal's species spirit and the Master of Animals, when they asked forgiveness for the act of killing it: an act that made the difficult, painful, brutal, yet also deeply holy and powerful business of life on earth possible.

That the Master of Animals did not die out in the Stone Age, but is alive today (and not just in his disguises as comic-book superheroes or movie monsters), is demonstrated by Otto Zerries in this narrative of a twentieth-century interaction between the Pygmies of Gabon and their version of the Master of Animals, who takes the form of an elephant named Khmwum.

Khmwum, writes Zerries, lives "in heaven and appears to humans as a rainbow in the eastern sky." He also manifests in dreams,

> appearing as a huge elephant who reports the location of an abundance of game. This gigantic elephant is called Gor, and he towers over the tallest tree in the forest. Blue in color, he supports the sky on his shoulders, and since he is immortal, no one can kill him. Gor is the chief of all the elephants; he is responsible for giving them life, and preserves them from the threat of extinction. He directs the elephants to those paths that the hunters take care to follow. A slain bull elephant is decorated with a bright blue liana, and the chief of the Pygmies dances on the carcass and sings to "father elephant." This is a solemn incantation in which the chief expresses the conviction that the elephant should not be outraged at being killed but pleased that he is going to the land of the spirits; he also says that the spear that erroneously took the elephant's life was misguided.

Here, in one fairly neat package, is all the guilt and all the glory, all the mingled beauty and horror that, for primitive humanity, the taking of animal life always implied. Even when they felt they had successfully received permission from its spirit, primordial peoples never felt totally at ease about taking an animal's life. A certain unavoidable aura of moral discomfort always hung over the act of hunting. The pygmies in this example obviously knew perfectly well that the spear that killed the elephant wasn't "misguided," but their desire to fudge the details to the Master of Animals reveals their basic complicity all the same.

For tens and even hundreds of thousands of years in variants past counting, this basic scenario unfolded again and again: emerging and submerging, sometimes being refined, sometimes being mangled almost beyond recognition, but ultimately always returning: a vision of a multitiered cosmos in which it is the job of both humans and animals, as soul-beings, to get along as best they can down here in the material world, and to keep fresh in memory that original world of spirit from which all life came and to which all life eventually returns. A world that once was identical to the physical world, but is now connected to it only in a few fragile places: a tree, a sacred mountain, or a rainbow bridge.

Mastery

From Animal to Vegetable

The rule of the Master of Animals was a long and stable one—the longest and most stable, in fact, in the history of humankind. Though life in the age of the hunter-collectors was far from perfect (indeed, by our modern standards it was often difficult, brutal, and short), from a spiritual perspective it had a certain essential *healthiness* to it: one that has inspired a note of wistful envy in many of those who have studied it from afar. "For a long period," wrote Edward Carpenter, "the tribes of men, like the tribes of the higher animals, must have been (on the whole, and allowing for occasional privations and sufferings and conflicts) well adapted to their surroundings and harmonious with the earth and with each other. There must have been a period resembling a Golden Age—some condition at any rate which, compared with subsequent miseries, merited the epithet 'golden.' "

Carpenter (who isn't too fashionable these days, but who was as valuable a source to me in my unraveling of the spiritual story of early humanity as Eliade, Joseph Campbell, and other, better-known writers), wrote those words in 1921, and though it may ring a little romantic to our ears, the contemporary nature writer Paul Shepard agrees with him. For some three million years, Shepard writes, "humankind was few in number, sensitive to the seasons and other life, humble in attitude toward the earth, and comfortable as one species among many. Group size was ideal for human relationships and human freedom, health was good despite (or perhaps because of!) high infant mortality rates, diet was in accord with our omnivorous physiology and sapient flexibility, and our ecology was stable and nonpolluting."

But by the end of the Paleolithic period, some ten thousand years ago, this easy balance between humans and the rest of nature began to slip. In Western Europe, with the warming of the climate and the retreat of the glaciers, humans emerged from the caves that had housed them during the centuries of the last ice age (during which all the great masterworks of cave art were created) and began to live out in the open. Wherever the glaciers retreated, securing game became much, much easier, and it appears that over the centuries that ease gave rise to a certain amount of ritual lassitude on the part of the ancient hunters. Wasteful hunting techniques in which whole herds of animals were driven off cliffs just to secure the meat from one or two of them took a severe toll on animal populations. In Europe, Russia, and eventually the Americas, entire species of prehistoric mammals—like the cave bear, the woolly mammoth, and the giant sloth—went extinct, in large part because of human predation.

Then—sometime after 10,000 BCE—came the invention of agriculture. Just as they had studied the movements and habits of animals for millennia, so humans now began to study plants. What they discovered was a whole new set of spiritual laws. No longer were the Master of Animals and the game herds he commanded the primary focus of the myths people told and the rituals they performed. Instead a new mythology grew up, centered on a new spiritual mystery: the one that occurred when a seed fell into the earth, died, and reemerged into the light.

A New Kind of God

As the spiritual life of the hunting societies had been focused on a supernatural figure that was at once human and animal, the planting societies were focused on one that was at once human and vegetable. Like the seed plants on which his life was modeled, this vegetable god was a child of his mother the earth (out of which he grew) and his father the sky (which nourished him with rain and sunlight). Also like those plants, his life was intimately tied to the cycle of the seasons. As the year turned and winter gave way to spring, the ancient agrarian festivals celebrated the miraculous birth of this vegetable god to his mother, the goddess of the earth. As the crops thickened in the summer months, stories were told of his youth and early manhood. Then, in the fall—when the days shortened and the time of harvest arrived—stories were told of his early and tragic death.

Winter was the time when this god of vegetation was most thoroughly and painfully absent. Dead and buried within the cold body of his mother, he became little more than a memory to the peoples who had celebrated him in the seasons of his strength. But just when the days were at their shortest and it seemed as if the vegetation would never again return, a shift occurred. Slowly but surely, the days grew longer. The sun grew in strength, the rains fell . . . and the vegetable god rose again.

Youthful by nature, the vegetable god was usually represented as either a baby nestled in the arms of his mother the earth, or as a beautiful, slightly feminine young man. Like the Master of Animals whose station in the human imagination he essentially replaced, the vegetable god could also appear, at times, as a woman. The Greek myth of the goddess Persephone, for example, who disappeared during the winter to live with Hades, the god of the underworld, is actually a story of the vegetable god in female guise. In Egypt, where the vegetable god was associated most strongly with corn, he was called Osiris. Cut to pieces and plowed into the ground by his brother Set, Osiris reassembled himself and rose back up into the light when his sister/wife, the goddess Isis, collected all the pieces and breathed life back into them. In Asia Minor he was Attis, a beautiful young shepherd beloved by the earth goddess Cybele, who was killed by a wound from a wild boar. Attis's death and resurrection were celebrated in the spring, and these rites survived from the far reaches of the early days of agriculture all the way into classical antiquity.

In *The Golden Bough*, Sir James George Frazer gives a description of the rites surrounding Attis's death and resurrection that could serve as a general description of the celebrations of the vegetable god that occurred everywhere in the ancient world. Writes Frazer of the final night of the period of mourning of the god's death:

> When night had fallen, the sorrow of the worshippers was turned to joy. For suddenly a light shone in the darkness: the tomb was opened: the god had risen from the dead; and as the priest touched the lips of the weeping

mourners with balm, he softly whispered in their ears the glad tidings of salvation. The resurrection of the god was hailed by his disciples as a promise that they too would issue triumphantly from the corruption of the grave. On the morrow, the twenty-sixth day of March, which was reckoned the vernal equinox, the divine resurrection was celebrated with a wild outburst of glee. At Rome, and probably elsewhere, the celebration took the form of a carnival. It was the festival of joy (*Hilaria*). A universal license prevailed. Every man might say and do what he pleased. People went about the streets in disguise. No dignity was too high or too sacred for the humblest citizen to assume with impunity.

The Ultimate Vegetation God

Many and marvelous as the vegetable god's manifestations were across the ancient world, his most miraculous incarnation of all did not occur until the dawn of our own era, when he appeared as neither god nor goddess but as a fully human baby, born to an equally human mother and father living in the Roman province of Galilee. So closely do Christ's life, death, and resurrection follow the pattern of the ancient agricultural gods that for a long time it was fashionable among scholars to suggest that Jesus wasn't a historical figure at all, but just a late—and largely unoriginal—addition to the virtually endless pantheon of similar young divinities who had been dying and resurrecting in the ancient world for thousands of years before his arrival. Jesus himself only encouraged this view when, in one of his most famous parables, he compared faith in the kingdom of heaven to a tiny mustard seed that falls into the earth, dies, and rises again as the mightiest of trees. That, after all, is the message of the vegetable god in a nutshell: die and sink into the earth like a plant, for like those plants you too will one day rise again.

But, these old scholarly arguments aside, to recognize in Jesus a model of the ancient agrarian gods isn't necessarily to discount the truth of either the Gospels or the message they contain. An argument can be made that the fact that Jesus' life took the pattern of a vegetation god's doesn't diminish the importance of Jesus so much as it provides the final demonstration of the centrality of vegetation imagery to the human spiritual imagination.

C. S. Lewis took this last idea a little further in his autobiographical account of his early years, *Surprised by Joy*. I discovered this book shortly after finishing my book on Mesoamerican myth, and it was the first time I encountered a writer who had made a compelling connection between Christianity (whose seeming dismissal of nature I'd found extremely troubling) and the primitive mythologies that spoke so much more appealingly to my imagination. Lewis had no qualms with the fact that Jesus' life so closely followed the pattern of the dying gods of the older religions. In fact, it even seemed to please him. *So what?* he asked in essence. Whether or not the earlier cults of the dying god represented, as he somewhat dismissively said, "the childhood of religion," and Christ represented its fulfillment, Lewis drove home for me the notion that whether one is a Christian or not, what matters is the strange organic integrity of the human religious impulse as it has unfolded over time. This appealed to me because the reason my whole quest had got going to begin with was the disconnect I experienced between Angus's death and the equipment my own culture had provided me for understanding it. As someone who had not grown up with an organic affinity toward Christianity, I was interested to find out if, going back far enough in time, I could find a place where its rites and literature might take on life for me. The story of the dying god gave me that link. Not only did it bring the Gospel stories to life; it also showed me how a religion I had previously believed had nothing to do with the natural world had had, way back in the past, *everything* to do with it. And this fact was nowhere more clearly in evidence than in Jesus' proclamation that the essential job of the soul, like the grain of wheat, was to die and be reborn.

The Wisdom of the Seed

As became ever more clear to me in my reading, if we are to understand what animals have meant to us over the course of history, we have to understand what vegetables mean as well; we also have to understand how the complex of spiritual meaning that grew up around the seed gradually disengaged itself from actual plants and became more abstract—so abstract that, entering a church today, we can very easily overlook the fact that we are entering a temple of the world's most successful vegetation cult.

The most influential figure in this transformation of seed wisdom from earthy realism to the more rarefied realms of theology was the apostle Paul, who wrote in First Corinthians,

But some will ask, "How are the dead raised? With what kind of body do they come?" You foolish man! What you sow does not come to life unless it dies. And what you sow is not the body which is to be, but a bare kernel, perhaps wheat or some other grain. But God gives it a body as he has chosen, and to each kind of seed its own body. For not all flesh is alike, but there is one kind for men, another for animals, another for birds, and another for fish. There are celestial bodies and there are terrestrial bodies; but the glory of the celestial is one, and the glory of the terrestrial is another. There is one glory of the sun, and another glory of the moon, and another glory of the stars; star differs from star in glory.

So it is with the resurrection of the dead. What is sown is perishable, what is raised is imperishable. It is sown in dishonor, it is raised in glory. It is sown in weakness, it is raised in power. It is sown in a physical body, it is raised in a spiritual body. If there is a physical body, there is also a spiritual body. Thus it is written, "The first man Adam became a living being": the last Adam became a life-giving spirit.

Before *Surprised by Joy,* passages like this were completely opaque and alien to me. But with Lewis's brief but illuminating remarks in mind, I began to see that the only way to unravel what had happened to the idea of the animal soul over history was to follow the plot all the way through, as it were, and look at the post-primitive religions—especially Christianity—as genuine continuations of the older nature religions. Doing so, I realized that much as it seemed not to be about nature and animals at all, Christianity was in fact the consummation of some six thousand years of wisdom derived from studying the spiritual nature of the seed; a wisdom that had in turn been born almost immediately at the conclusion of that vast chapter of human history and prehistory when animals had been the center of all of humankind's deepest spiritual concerns.

Into the Corral

The Christian concept of a spiritual resurrection body was a natural, almost inevitable outgrowth of the agricultural religions that had preceded it. In Christianity (in the Gospels but especially in Paul) the "living being"—the *nephesh chaya* that God created in Genesis when he breathed spirit into the earth-molded body of Adam—died and transformed at last into a truly immortal being: one no longer at the mercy of life or life's seasons, for like the stars in the sky above it lived forever. But there was another force at work in this new incarnation of the concept of *nephesh* as well: one that came not from the Hebrew world but from ancient Greece. Christianity was born from a unique marriage of Greek and Hebrew conceptions of the soul. For the Greeks—and most especially Plato—the idea that the soul could exist free of the body was a perfectly sound and sensible one. But for the Hebrews, a soul without a body made no sense (which is why, as we will shortly see, the Hebrew Bible is highly pessimistic about the existence of the human soul after death in anything but a pathetically reduced form). Paul solved this problem by positing a body that was at once physical yet more-than-physical. A body that, like a seed, was sown in the corruption of earth, only to die and transform into a body that was not so much immaterial as *more* than material.

Which (at last) gets the story back to animals proper. On the heels of the invention of agriculture came animal husbandry—the keeping of domesticated beasts that could be milked, sheared, or slaughtered and eaten at human convenience. (We're talking, here, about livestock animals like oxen and pigs. Dogs—a special case—entered human company long before other animals did, possibly as long ago as 30,000 BCE.) It used to be thought that the decision to domesticate animals was a fairly deliberate one on the part of our forebears. But anthropologists and archaeologists have recently begun to take a different view of the matter. It now appears that humans may not have played nearly the direct, conscious role in the process of domestication that scientists once believed they did. Only certain animals take readily to domestication, and the decision on the part of those animals to join the company of humans now seems to have played just as big a role in the process of domestication as did the efforts of the humans who gradually brought those animals into the human fold.

The historian Richard W. Bulliet suggests that while the original thinking on the domestication of animals like the ancestors of today's pigs, sheep, and chickens was that it was a sudden and ingenious inspiration on the part of one or more early humans, it now appears much more likely that the process happened almost of itself over the centuries, without the humans involved even being fully aware of what was going on. The beginning of domestication, Bulliet suggests, "probably attracted little notice when it was occurring. When the first wild animals were being penned or tolerated as they skulked around the campsite catching mice or scavenging garbage, no one knew that ox-drawn plows, horse-drawn chariots, pinstriped wool suits, frozen yogurt, and Kentucky Fried Chicken were looming in the distant future."

Another surprising aspect of domestication that is just coming to light is the reason it may initially have appealed to the people involved. Looking back from our perspective, it's easy to imagine that a few village dwellers one day simply decided to fence in some cows or pigs so that they could have a constant food source available instead of having to go out and procure them by hunting. But Bulliet suggests that food, important as it was, may not have been the initial draw of domestication. The first domesticated animals, Bulliet believes, were welcomed into the human fold not so much for the ready supply of food they provided, but because humans needed a constant supply of live animals to sacrifice.

Unlike the animal gods that had preceded them, the new agricultural gods demanded more than simple praise and respect. In order to receive life—in the form of crops—humans needed to *give* life, and (not surprisingly) the lives they preferred to give were those of animals. As villages grew into towns and towns into cities, the earth's planting peoples were increasingly dependent on reliable crops to feed their swelling populations. A bad harvest meant starvation, but it also meant the possible revolt of a city's subjects against the rulers who had failed them by angering the gods of earth and sky. To prevent hunger and strife, sacrificial payments needed to be made, and made regularly.

"The meat from a sacrifice," writes Bulliet, "is eaten. The

patron or sponsor of the sacrifice gives it away freely after special portions of the slaughtered animal have been offered to the
gods, the officiating priests, or other specially entitled parties."
By sacrificing a captive animal, the patron of the sacrifice could
make himself look good before both his family and peers, and
before the gods to whom the sacrifice was made.

Holy Power on Tap

The *Manitou*—the holy power that animals possessed—and
particularly the large amounts of that holy power that came into
play when an animal left its body to return to the spirit world,
became in the agricultural age something it had never been in
the age of the hunter-gatherers: a commodity. A ready supply
of captive animals was not only a convenient source of food to
these early planting communities but a ready supply of holiness
that could be drawn on, like a stack of firewood behind one's
house, whenever the occasion demanded.

It was easy enough for me to see how damaging this new
spiritual economy must have been to the human ability to per-
ceive animals as fellow soul beings. Over the millennia during
which our ancient forebears had survived by hunting and gathering, animals had been spiritual equals—possessors of a soul
life that rendered them, beneath the skin, different from but not
inferior to humans. But with the dawn of the planting cultures
and the new agricultural spiritual universe that grew up with it,
animals went from kindred souls and fellow traders within the
larger economy of spirit to simple possessions: important but

essentially inferior beings that we could use for our material or spiritual benefit, whenever and however we wished.

Animals were the first true property. The words *cattle* and *capital* derive from the same root, and the fact that the first letter in our alphabet is an upside-down representation of a cow's head is a keen reminder that writing itself most likely originated out of the need to keep track of how many cattle the wealthy members of the earth's first cities possessed. Animals didn't lose *all* their old holy power with the rise of the first cities. The bull, in particular, remained a living embodiment of the sacred for the ancient cities of the Near East just as it had been for the cave artists of the Paleolithic. (The walls of the main temple at the city of Çatal Hüyük in present-day Anatolia, at nine thousand years the single oldest religious shrine in the world, is decorated with the massive heads of broad-horned bulls; Apis, the creator god of the ancient Egyptians, took the form of a bull as well.) But though still sacred creatures, the bulls, lions, he-goats, and other animals illustrated by artists in ancient Near Eastern cities like Sumer and Ur were in essence symbolic of *human* power (be it worldly or spiritual or both) more than embodiments of sacred animal power in and of itself.

Egypt appears to have maintained a respect for the spiritual potency of animals without completely subsuming that power to political or economic (i.e., human) concerns for much longer than other ancient civilizations did. But even it was ultimately unable to keep animals and their unique holy power free from the machineries of urban agricultural existence. Though the Egyptians never stopped both loving animals and celebrating them for their sacred power, in Egypt, too, these animals ultimately failed to manifest the pure spiritual force that they had for the ancient hunting peoples. If that force survived at all, it did so in the royal hunt, where Egypt's kings would hunt animals celebrated for their beauty, bravery, and spiritual power. But no matter how brave or beautiful the lions, leopards, and hoofed animals look in the Egyptian paintings and stone relief sculptures of these hunts, it is the Egyptian rulers in their chariots, looming imposingly above their prey with their arrows drawn back, who are the true heroes of the drama. The animals, through their deaths, only serve to shine further glory on their royal killers.

Gilgamesh

One of the clearest descriptions of the loss of mystery and power that animals suffered with the shift from hunting to agriculture occurs in the story of Gilgamesh, a half-historical, half-mythic hero of the Sumerians, a people who inhabited Mesopotamia around 5000 BCE. The Sumerians were among the earth's first true city builders. Their sizable populations depended on irrigation, extensive grain storage, and other sophisticated farming techniques that had taken thousands of years to perfect. Hunters and gatherers the Sumerians very definitely weren't, yet they were close enough to that ancient heritage that a memory of the shift from hunting to farming, and the change in spiritual attitude that came along with it, is clearly evident in their myths and epics.

In the story, Gilgamesh is a great king who clashes with a figure named Enkidu. "His body was rough," we read of Enkidu, "he had long hair like a woman's; it waved like the hair of

Nisaba, the goddess of corn. His body was covered with matted hair like Samuqan's, the god of cattle. He was innocent of mankind; he knew nothing of the cultivated land."

Neither wholly man nor wholly beast, "Enkidu ate grass in the hills with the gazelle and lurked with wild beasts at the water-holes; he had joy of the water with the herds of wild game." One of Enkidu's great pleasures was to destroy the traps that humans set for game in the wilderness, and to release the animals trapped within them. One day out in the wild, Enkidu encounters one of these trappers face-to-face. Terrified, the trapper returns to his home and tells his father what he has seen.

"Father, there is a man, unlike any other, who comes down from the hills. He is the strongest in the world, he is like an immortal from heaven. He ranges over the hills with wild beasts and eats grass; he ranges through your land and comes down to the wells. I am afraid and dare not go near him."

The trapper's father tells him to go to the capital city of Uruk and speak to Gilgamesh. "Extol the strength of this wild man," the trapper's father says. "Ask him to give you a harlot, a wanton from the temple of love; return with her, and let her woman's power overpower this man. When next he comes down to drink at the wells she will be there, stripped naked; and when he sees her beckoning he will embrace her, and then the wild beasts will reject him."

So it happens. Returning from his encounter with the woman to the beasts of the field, Enkidu receives a cruel shock. "Then, when the gazelle saw him, they bolted away; when the wild creatures saw him they fled. Enkidu would have followed, but his body was bound as though with a cord, his knees gave way when

he started to run, his swiftness was gone. And now the wild creatures had all fled away; Enkidu was grown weak, for wisdom
was in him, and the thoughts of a man were in his heart."

Though Enkidu's loss of primordial innocence is to some extent a parallel of the story of Adam and Eve and their own sexu-
ally tinged fall from the original happiness of paradise, it is also
directly related to animals, and the new relationship humans
had with animals in the age of agriculture. Enkidu, with his long,
flowing hair and his easy commerce with the beasts of the wa-
tering hole, is clearly a holdover from earlier times, when humans interacted more directly with animals on a spiritual level.
There are strong hints of the Master of Animals in him, and his
transformation through his introduction into human company is
in essence a distillation of what happened to humans themselves
when they strayed out of the company of the Master of Animals
and into the embrace of agriculture.

Enkidu's fall was, it was easy for me to see by now, the fall of
all humanity in the agricultural age. The "wisdom" of humans
no longer allowed them to commune directly with animals and
the spiritual realm from which they came. As the first great agricultural cities rose up in the sands of the Near East, animals
underwent the final stage of their transformation from fellow
spirits to mere possessions.

The Laws of the Pastoralists

There are two basic ways of herding cattle: by keeping them in
a stationary location, or by wandering with them. The first way
demands wealth—primarily in terms of land on which to house

and feed one's animals. The second demands that a people be mobile enough to travel along with their herds as they move from place to place, wherever the grazing is best.

Farmers and pastoralists have, it seems, always been somewhat suspicious of each other. To the pastoralist, the life of the farmer is cramped and constrained. To the farmer, whose gods, laws, and very sense of self are wedded to the land he works, the wandering pastoralist is a person without a face, his laws incomprehensible and his gods untrustworthy.

Around 1000 BCE, a group of wandering herders with a greater-than-average prejudice against the agricultural mentality (and the religions of blood sacrifice that went along with it) appeared amid the empire-builders of the Near East. Single, all-powerful, moody but essentially benevolent (especially toward the people through whom he had chosen to make his word known upon the earth), the sky-god worshipped by the Hebrews was not, like so many of the gods before him, a mixture of human and animal qualities, but human and human alone. Agriculturalists tended to be liberal in their tolerance of other peoples' gods. Pastoralists were less so, and the Hebrews proved to be the culture least tolerant of other peoples' gods that the world had yet seen. In addition to condemning every one of the countless agricultural deities (that is, nature gods) worshipped by their neighbors, the Hebrews introduced a new set of moral proscriptions to humankind—a charter for the things people could and could not do down on the plane of earth. Here were laws in which the individual human being mattered as he (and, to a degree, she) had never mattered before.

These laws applied not just to people, but to the rest of

creation as well. Though animals and humans were very definitely *not* equal in the Hebrew mind, all animals—even the most unsavory ones—were God's creations: carriers of *nephesh*, the life essence breathed into Adam at the start of the world. And as God made it very clear in Genesis that all of his creation was good, all animals deserved a certain minimal measure of respect as parts of it.

Like any herding people, the Hebrews spent more time thinking about livestock than they did about other animals, and they devoted as much time establishing a code of conduct regarding them as they did every other central aspect of their lives. "When an ox gores a man or a woman to death," advises Deuteronomy, "the ox shall be stoned, and its flesh shall not be eaten; but the owner of the ox shall be clear. But if the ox has been accustomed to gore in the past, and its owner has been warned but has not kept it in, and it kills a man or a woman, the ox shall be stoned and its owner also shall be put to death. If a ransom is laid on him, then he shall give for the redemption of his life whatever is laid upon him. If it gores a man's son or daughter, he shall be dealt with according to this same rule. If the ox gores a slave, male or female, the owner shall give to their master thirty shekels of silver, and the ox shall be stoned."

While it was precisely passages like this that had long troubled me about the Hebrew Bible—just as they have so many other modern readers with an interest in connecting with the natural world instead of objectifying and dominating it—it's a good idea to remember that along with ownership-centered passages like these, the Hebrew Bible is replete with many a passage describing the glories of God's creation in tones of poetic admiration.

"In wisdom you made them all," we read in Psalms, "the earth is full of your creatures. There is the sea, vast and spacious, teeming with creatures beyond number—living things both large and small. . . . When you send your Spirit, they are created and you renew the earth."

And this, from Job: "But ask the beasts, and they will teach you; the birds of the air and they will tell you; or the plants of the earth, and they will teach you; and the fish of the sea will declare to you. Who among these does not know that the hand of the Lord has done this? In his hand is the life of every living thing and the breath of all mankind."

It's also important to keep in mind that the covenant God establishes with Noah after the floodwaters have withdrawn is one with *all* creation, not just humans. A basic respect for the value of animal creation runs throughout the Hebrew Bible, and that respect always contains at least a modicum of concern for the well-being of the animal itself. "A righteous man," says Proverbs 12, "has regard for the life of his beast." The animals with which the Hebrews shared their world were pieces of God's handiwork, and as such deserved the respect due all of God's creation.

But, cheerful as all this is, if we weigh all the books of the Hebrew Bible together, the fact remains that in it, animals are very definitely beings that exist on a qualitative level *beneath* that of humans. Though the Hebrews were absorbed as no people before them had been with the issue of nationhood, animal creation did not constitute such a nation in their minds. The Master of Animals, in other words, is nowhere to be found in the Hebrew Bible. In archaic times humans and animals had lived together under the roof of a heaven that had retreated from the world but was still, essentially, within reach. But now, as the sole and single God of the Hebrews took over the rule of heaven, all focus centered on the one and only being down on earth that had been made in his image. At the dawn of the Judeo-Christian era, animals had become what they in essence were to remain until the arrival of the modern world in the late nineteenth and early twentieth centuries: beings created by God for human use, with only a very secondary spiritual existence.

Souls, Human and Otherwise

> The fate of humans and the fate of animals is the same; as one dies, so dies the other. They all have the same breath, and humans have no advantage over the animals; for all is vanity. All go to one place; all are from the dust, and all turn to dust again.
>
> —*Ecclesiastes*

As should be apparent by now—and as I myself slowly discovered in the course of my Angus-inspired investigations—there is no way to understand what people have thought about the animal soul over history and prehistory without first understanding what they thought of the human soul and its relation to the divine. One day while writing this book, I rented a U-Haul van to move some of my possessions from my wife's and my apartment in New York City out to our house on Long Island. The woman who ran the U-Haul place had two dogs with her. One was a small white mixed breed that, as we arranged for my rental, stood on her desk and issued a continuous series of lively, if not entirely unfriendly, barks. In the woman's lap was another dog, slightly larger, that had lost most of the fur on its body.

"How old is she?" I asked, motioning to the dog on her lap.

"Fifteen," the woman said. "She sits on my lap all day because she gets upset if I leave her. I had to put another of my dogs down last year and it pretty near killed *me*. I'm not looking forward to when this girl leaves me. So what are you picking up in the city?"

"Books mostly," I said. "I have way too many of them. Actually, I'm writing a book right now on whether animals have souls or not."

The woman paused in filling out her paperwork.

"Whether they have *souls* or not?" she asked, as if trying the idea on for size. "Well, I guess some folks believe they don't. Of course, there's some out there who don't even think *people* have souls!"

It might be a good idea to keep that comment in mind during the portion of our investigation that follows. For in fact there *are* people out there—plenty of them—who believe that not only animals but people, too, lack souls. And if we are to arrive at an informed opinion as to why they just might be wrong about *animals* not having souls, we require a detour of sorts into some of the thornier questions that arose in the past about the human soul—especially in the two countries that between them are the parents of almost all the Western world's spiritual ideas: ancient Greece and Israel.

Beliefs about the human soul in ancient times were often surprisingly different from what we might imagine. To begin with, ancient cultures typically believed that human beings had not just one but several souls. There was a "free" soul (the equivalent of the Greek *psyche* and the Hebrew *nephesh*) that journeyed out of the body when a person was asleep (and that left for good when a person died) and a "body" soul that took over when a person was awake. The body soul, in turn, comprised two or three different parts, each one of which was located in a different part of the body and connected with a specific mental or physical process.

Weird as this all sounds to us, it was much less so in a world where the brain had yet to receive unquestioned status as the organ of human thought. Ancient peoples took these various and sundry souls very much for granted, and saw them at work in the most ordinary activities. Sneezing, for example, was seen as a soul event in many ancient cultures—and a dangerous one, for it could actually rocket one's psyche out of one's head for a moment (which is one reason why, when a person sneezes today, it is still customary to offer a blessing).

How many of these souls could animals possess? All of them—at least according to the cultures that retained strong connections to the animistic past. Early Greek philosophers like Pythagoras, and early Greek philosophical systems like Orphism (named after Orpheus, the shamanic lyre-playing hero who we saw had connections with the Master of Animals), not only believed that animals had souls, but that, as the Buddhists and Hindus also believed, an individual soul could reincarnate in human, animal, or even plant form. (These early Greek notions of reincarnation/metempsychosis may have been borrowed, at least in part, from Eastern sources, for contact between ancient Greece and India is now thought to have been quite significant.) Jan N. Bremmer reports that the Greek philosopher Empedocles "specifically forbade the chewing of laurel leaves, since he regarded the laurel as the highest form of plant incarnations, and even claimed to have been a bush himself in a previous existence."

What is most important about these early Greek philosophies (just as it is with those of the East) is their willingness to grant a genuinely spiritual consciousness to beings *other* than humans. For the Orphics and the Pythagoreans, life *always* entailed the existence of soul, and the shape and character of that soul was secondary to the fact that all physical life was irreducibly spiritual in nature.

But once again, as we saw with the Far East, *spiritual* doesn't necessarily mean *personal*. In the case of ancient Greece, that distinction is especially evident as we move out of the esoteric world of the Orphics and Pythagoreans and encounter the more popular beliefs about the soul represented in Homer and the Greek tragedians.

The World of Shadows

When we in the modern Western world hear the word *soul*, we immediately connect it with personality. Our soul, we sense, is what gives each of us that feeling of mysteriously particular, unrepeatable *me*-ness—of being, beneath our names and our histories and the roles we play in the world, something more than all these things: something that, indefinable as it is, *soul* somehow manages to conjure best.

As we saw earlier, the word *psyche* carried similar associations for most of classical antiquity (that is, the thousand or so years of civilization centering around the Mediterranean leading up to the birth of Jesus at the start of our era) just as the word *nephesh* did in the Near East for the Hebrews during this same general period. But—and this is the most important part—these words only carried those associations during the time that an individual was alive on earth. Ancient Greece and Israel virtually created, between them, the modern idea of human individuality. From the Hebrew Bible and the great works of Greek drama and philosophy come the vast majority of the ideas about how to value, nurture, and define the individual human person to which we continue to subscribe today. Both cultures were also responsible for many of the beliefs about the soul and spirit that we continue to entertain, or half entertain, here in the modern world. But for both these cultures, the ultimate fate of the soul—that is, what happens to it when it leaves the body permanently at death— was surprisingly bleak.

Both the Hebrews and the Greeks focused their afterlife beliefs not on a heavenly upper world but on a grim and gloomy underworld. While the various body souls simply perished at death, the *psyche* or *nephesh* escaped from the body and traveled to the underworld (which the Greeks called Hades and the Hebrews called Sheol). Once there, it transformed into a new kind of being: one that both Greece and Israel described as a "shade." (The word is *repha'im* in Hebrew, *skia* in Greek.)

The afterlife enjoyed by these Greek and Hebrew shades was a far from enviable one. "In the noontide of my days I must depart," says Isaiah,

I am consigned to the gates of Sheol for the rest of my years.
I said, I shall not see the Lord in the land of the living:
I shall look upon man no more among the inhabitants of the
  world . . .
For Sheol cannot thank you, death cannot praise you;
those who go down to the Pit cannot hope for your faithfulness.

Not even God, this passage suggests, can reach far enough down to help the souls of the dead languishing in Sheol. The authors of other books of the Bible felt the same way. "In death there is no remembrance of you," we read in Psalms, while Samuel reminds us that "we must all die; we are like water spilled on the ground, which cannot be gathered up."

So it was over in ancient Greece as well. When Achilles, in the twenty-third book of the *Iliad,* meets the shade of his old friend Patroclus one night in a dream, it is not the man he knew in life that he discovers, but a dim, diminished, cardboard cutout who can barely remember what life on earth was like at all.

There came to him the spirit of hapless Patroclus, in all things like his very self, in stature and fair eyes and in voice, and in like raiment was he clad withal; and he stood above Achilles' head and spake to him, saying: "Thou sleepest, and hast forgotten me, Achilles. Not in my life wast thou unmindful of me, but now in my death!"

Achilles held out his arms to clasp the spirit, but in vain. It vanished like a wisp of smoke and went gibbering underground. Achilles leapt up in amazement. He beat his hands together and in his desolation cried: "Ah then, it is true that something of us does survive even in the Halls of Hades, but with no intellect at all, only the ghost and semblance of a man."

Love, laughter, companionship—for both the ancient Hebrew and the ancient Greek, these were joys of the living, and for the living alone. To die was, if not to vanish entirely, to become less—much less—than what one had been while alive on earth. Like over-medicated patients on a mental ward, the shades of the dead either sleep or wander about endlessly and pointlessly, scarcely remembering their life on earth or the people and things they had known and loved while there.

Just as most primitive hunting cultures felt a degree of guilt over the act of hunting because they knew it was essentially an activity that had not taken place before the fall out of the world of spirit, so most primitive peoples felt some fear of the human dead: a fear that was unavoidable given the mystery and invisibility of the land to which the departed soul traveled. Even in primitive societies where the afterworld was viewed as an entirely positive place, precautions were often taken with the newly dead (tying their limbs, burying them beneath large rocks) to ensure that their souls stayed where they belonged and didn't try to sneak back into the world of the living once they were gone.

Though primitive religious thought harbored doubt and fear about the afterlife, the singularly grim visions of it entertained by Greece and Israel marked a definite—and disturbing—detour from the path that primordial humanity had laid out. At the start of Western culture as we know it, there lay a vision of the life beyond that was so uniformly depressing that it is scarcely even possible to connect it to the more positive visions held by so many primitive cultures. A character in Euripides' play *Meleagros* sums up as well as anyone the situation for the souls of the dead in both ancient Greece and Israel: "After death every man is earth and shadow: nothing goes to nothing."

Heaven for Philosophers

But of course, if this is how the afterlife began in Western culture, it is not how it remained. What changed the Western vision of the afterlife from that of a dim and hopeless twilight zone into the land of glory and fulfillment that the word *heaven* conjures up for us today? The first real rustlings of this change began in the Greek mystery schools—those carefully guarded secret societies that flourished in a number of Greek cities from the sixth century BCE till the early centuries of our own era. In the Eleusinian Mysteries—the longest-lived and most important of these mystery schools—initiates ate a communion-like cake made of cornmeal and underwent a mystical death-and-resurrection experience that allowed them to feel that, like the vegetable goddess Persephone who went down to the underworld but later returned from it, he or she had tasted death and been reborn.

The mystery schools operated on the very old and widespread premise that while the soul is *potentially* immortal, it requires certain procedures in order for this immortality to kick in properly. Through initiation into the mystery cult, the human soul is not only able to survive death, but to survive it *personally*. Not only does it have an unambiguously positive place to go to, but it is allowed to bring with it that essential piece of carry-on luggage that, in earlier Greek visions of the afterlife, it had been forced to leave behind: the full and complete sense of self that made humans truly human in the first place.

Important as they were to those fortunate souls who took part in them, the larger impact of the mystery schools was limited by their members' extreme secrecy, and the primarily emotional rather than intellectual impact of the rites themselves. If an initiate in the mysteries came away no longer fearing his or her own death, that did not mean he or she possessed a philosophy about life that could be shared with others.

Then, in the fifth century BCE, came Plato. Together with his teacher Socrates, Plato completely revolutionized the Western view of death. Rather than a gloomy underworld of muttering, amnesiac shadows, Plato envisioned Hades as a light-filled wonderland: a place where earthly imperfections (and what was there on earth, when you got down to it, that wasn't imperfect in some way or other?) were thoroughly and triumphantly left behind. In place of all the flawed, incompletely realized beings and objects that bumped and bungled about down on the plane of physical existence, the Platonic heaven contained only perfect, nonphysical objects: the Forms. Basically an updated version of the primitive idea of the species spirit (as we mentioned before in conjunction with the Paleolithic cave paintings), the Forms were spiritual models for everything found on earth, from living beings to inanimate objects.

This land of spiritualized perfection, Plato also said, is our only true country. Throughout the course of its earthly existence, the soul secretly longs to be reunited with the perfection of heaven. "For Plato," writes the New Testament scholar N. T. Wright, "the soul is the non-material aspect of a human being, and is the aspect that really matters. Bodily life is full of delusion and danger; the soul is to be cultivated in the present both for its own sake and because its future happiness will depend on such cultivation. The soul, being immortal, existed before the body, and will continue to exist after the body is gone. Since for many Greeks 'the immortals' were the gods, there is always the suggestion, at least by implication, that human souls are in some way divine."

Can These Bones Live?

If there is anything negative about the Platonic version of the afterlife, it is that it is just ever so slightly . . . sterile. Plato's afterlife was a realm of pure thought, a place incalculably brighter, better, and more real than earthly existence ever could be. But because of its completely immaterial nature, it was also bloodless and pale. Even at its warmest, Plato's heaven always remained just a little bit cold—much too cold to fully satisfy the human desire for an afterlife encompassing the full range of human emotion, and too cold as well to satisfy my own desire for an afterlife that embraced both people and animals in all their living individuality.

It struck me as an odd coincidence that the human element I found so noticeably missing from Plato's vision of the soul and the afterlife was increasingly a subject of discussion right across the Mediterranean at just about the time he was composing his dialogues. Just as they had among the Greeks, changes were occurring in the Hebrew view of the life beyond the body. And these changes proved to carry just the ingredient that the bright, promising, but disappointingly abstract world of the Platonic afterlife needed in order to fill it out.

What was this missing ingredient? The body. Not the purely physical body that broke, got sick, and eventually died down on the plane of earth, but the *spiritual* body. Though for the great majority of its pages the Hebrew Bible entertains a consistently negative picture of the afterlife, in the later books certain passages appear that suggest a very different fate for the soul: a new kind of postmortem existence that is neither simply physical nor simply spiritual, but both at once.

"The hand of the Lord was upon me," writes Ezekiel, "and carried me out in the spirit of the Lord, and set me down in the midst of the valley which was full of bones, and caused me to pass by them round about: and, behold, there were very many in the open valley; and, lo, they were very dry. And he said unto me, Son of man, can these bones live? And I answered, O Lord God, thou knowest."

Warmth, depth, and personality in all its complex, Technicolor richness: for most of the Hebrew Bible, all these qualities vanished at death. But in Ezekiel's vision, something else seems to be going on. He witnesses a return—a restoration—in which death is overcome, and in which, miraculously, the dead arise as the full, flesh-and-blood people they had originally been.

This vision of Ezekiel's is a pointedly political metaphor; it suggests that the Jewish nation, which had been scattered and laid low by the hand of history, would one day rise and cohere again. The several other resurrection passages in the Hebrew

Bible relate to political renewal as well, but they are also talking about another kind of renewal, the kind that happens when a dead person actually returns to life. Proclaims Isaiah:

> *Your dead shall live, their corpses shall rise,*
> *O dwellers in the dust, awake and sing for joy!*
> *For your dew is a radiant dew,*
> *and the earth will give birth to those long dead.*

Least ambiguous of all is the following, from the latest book in the Hebrew Bible, the Book of Daniel:

"Many of those who sleep in the dust of the earth shall awake, some to everlasting life, and some to shame and everlasting contempt. Those who are wise shall shine like the brightness of the sky, and those who lead many to righteousness, like the stars for ever and ever."

No one knows precisely how the seemingly eccentric notion of bodily resurrection made its way into Hebrew thought. But however the Jews did come upon it, the idea that a living being could resurrect itself (and, in the lines of Ezekiel, resurrect itself from its bones) was not original to them. Bequeathed by the hunters of the Paleolithic, it is the kind of idea that could only be hatched by a people who were neither exclusively materialistic (the only true life is the life of the body) nor exclusively spiritualistic (the only true life is the life of the soul). To envision a human actually returning to full life and consciousness from his bones, one must respect the world of matter *and* the world of spirit equally.

And though we can never know it for certain, it seems very

likely that the earth's first peoples did just that. Heaven—the earth above the earth, where the souls of humans and animals traveled when they left their bodies behind—was not, for them, a wasteland full of ghostly shades, nor was it a cerebral, abstract realm of perfect but bloodless ideas. It was instead a heaven in the fullest and richest sense of the word: a place so tied to earth that when earthly creatures died and entered it, they left a portion of their immortal, imperishable selves behind in the form of bones—bones that, when the time was right, could magically re-clothe themselves with flesh.

Though Judaism started out as a religion that was theoretically unconcerned with the fate of the individual at death, the Hebrews were becoming, as the birth of Jesus approached, a people ever more interested in questions of individual survival—of what would happen not just to the Jewish nation, but to the soul of the individual person when it left the body behind. In Greece, meanwhile, the Platonic heaven of perfect, abstract forms lay as if waiting for someone to breathe a little more earthly life into it—to make it a place not just of perfection, but of fully personal, fully *human* perfection.

In both Greece and the Near East, a new vision of the soul was ready to come to birth: one in which the ancient hunter's idea that the body can resurrect itself from its bones, and the ancient farmer's idea that the soul was like a grain of wheat that falls into the earth, dies, and rises again, would meet and magically mingle. In this new vision, neither the blessings of the physical body nor those of the spiritual soul were to be completely lost at death, for the seemingly exclusive categories of body and soul were to be transcended through the birth of a *spiritual body*:

one that, far from being a ghostly phantom, was infinitely more real and substantial than the fallen, purely earthly body that had preceded it on earth.

What was the form this new vision finally took? And—most important for our purposes—what did this new school of thinking have to say not just about the human soul, but about the *animal* soul as well?

The answer to the first question is obvious. The name of the new spiritual vision that so daringly and fruitfully combined Greek and Hebrew speculation about the nature of body and soul was Christianity.

But answering the second question, I discovered, proved a little more difficult.

The Rational Animal

The hand of the Lord has not neglected the bodies of
the smallest animals—and still less their souls.
—*Origen (c. CE 185–254), Commentary on Psalm 1*

It may seem strange—for Christians no less than for anybody else—to envision Christianity as a religion that fulfilled the promise of Paleolithic spirituality. But that, I discovered, is exactly what Christianity managed to do—at least for a time. "The Greek tradition about the soul," writes John A. Sanford, "especially as mediated through the mystery religions and through Plato, flowered in the Christian idea of the soul." And the roots of that metaphorical flower reached back not to the Greeks but farther back—all the way back, in fact, to the Stone Age.

Why did early Christianity fulfill the Paleolithic promise? Because it returned heaven to what it had originally been: a place where earthly life—*all* of earthly life—was welcome. With Christianity the intellectual advances of the Greek genius and the moral advances of the Hebrew genius joined together to create a vision of the soul in which not only was the inner "me"—the irreducibly particular person, with all of his or her loves and hates, memories and hopes and dreams and desires— rescued from death and oblivion, but the entire natural world was as well.

This may be news to the many who, as I long did, think of Christianity as the quintessential anti-nature religion. God's mandate to Adam and Eve to "subdue" nature and exercise "dominion" over it—words that allowed some less inspired Hebrews to believe that all animals were placed before them for their use—was, as everybody knows, intensified by Christian thought into a view of nature that made it not just secondary to humanity, but downright evil. Out there in the darkness of nature, much of Christian literature tells us, dwells the Devil. Because of this, the justification for the Western project of dominating and destroying the natural world has been laid squarely at Christianity's feet.

All this is, unfortunately, true. But it turns out that another, less remarked-upon stream within the Christian tradition says just the opposite. "As for those who are far from God," wrote the Greek Church Father Evagrius of Pontus, "God has made it possible for them to come near to the knowledge of him through the medium of creatures. These he has produced, as the letters of the alphabet, so to speak, by his power and his wisdom." Central to the Christian message is the idea that the *Logos,* or word of God, has been sown like a seed into all of creation. By learning what the Greek prayer text the *Philokalia* calls the "language" of created life, according to certain voices within the early Church we can learn, as the Church Father Origen declares, that "the word is present in every creature, however small."

Gone, in this line of Christian thought, is the image of the human being as the sole earthly embodiment of God's wisdom that runs through so much of Jewish and Christian thought. In its place is a vision in which the human being is central, but in which, Orpheus-like, he stands beneath the shade of the cosmic tree with the species spirits of the world's animals assembled all around him.

"It could even be," wrote Origen, "that God who made the human race 'in his own image and likeness' also gave to other creatures a likeness to certain celestial realities. Perhaps this resemblance is so detailed that even the grain of mustard seed has its counterpart in the kingdom of heaven. And if that is true for seeds it must be the same for plants. And if it is true of plants it cannot be otherwise for animals, birds, reptiles and four-footed beasts."

Beyond suggesting that all of earthly creation matters to God, Origen is restating, in Christian terms, the ancient idea that heaven is not some bloodless, abstract mental zone where only mental realities are welcome, but a second earth, one where all the creatures that we know on earth continue to exist in a spiritualized form that erases nothing of their earthly individuality. "It may be granted," Origen continues, "that these creatures, seeds, plants, roots and animals, are undoubtedly at the service of humanity's physical needs. However, they include the shape and image of the invisible world, and they also have the task of elevating the soul and guiding it to the contemplation of celestial objects." Here was a message that I, animal-loving, confused, and disaffected member of the nominally Christian world that I was, could relate to completely. Though we have to make use of animals and plants to survive down here in the physical world, this line of Christian thinking declares that doesn't mean we need to ignore the divine, celestial light that is hiding within every one of them after all.

A Place for All Creation

The heaven described by many of the early Church Fathers was, remarkably, a heaven not of clouds and halos—or not *just* of clouds and halos—but of plants and animals as well: plants and animals that have lost not one iota of their earthly charm and particularity by leaving the terrestrial world behind. "Wisdom," writes the Church Father Maximus the Confessor, "consists in seeing every object in accordance with its true nature." And while human and animal "wisdom" certainly differed, all beings carried a measure of wisdom appropriate to their nature—as I had discovered the primitives knew so well from watching the animals around them build their perfect nests and houses, and move with perfect assurance across the earth.

Perhaps the most surprising (and reassuring) thing to me about this supremely nature-friendly school of Christian thought was that it was echoed in other faiths as well. Jewish thought underwent a series of transformations of its own during those early years of the Christian Church, and Jewish mystical schools developed their own maps of the multileveled cosmos, such as the Sephirothic tree of the Kabbalah, which places the earth, and physical life in general, within a hierarchy of worlds, at the top of which is a God who, at the end of incarnate existence, will welcome all of creation back into himself. (For, as the Talmud states, "this whole world is merely a vestibule for the world to come.") In Islam, meanwhile, which possessed a strong mystical element from its very beginnings in the seventh century, the earth-above-the-earth was known as the Earth of Visions, and all of nature, down to the smallest plant and the most seemingly insignificant creature, was thought to have its true spiritual existence there, just as Origen describes the creatures of the Christian heaven doing. The distinction between science and religion that has become so pronounced in the modern West was, I discovered, never a part of Islam, and many of its greatest sages, like the twelfth-century philosopher and scientist Avicenna, devoted their lives to uncovering the connections between nature and spirit, the visible and invisible aspects of creation. Islam's inclusive view of nature is everywhere apparent in the Koran, where it is repeatedly affirmed that Allah is both "the light of the heavens and the earth," (24:34) and that "all creatures celebrate His praises" (17:44). Islam's respect for animal creation specifically, meanwhile, is evidenced in the Koran's admonishments to treat one's animals decently, and in its belief that nature itself is a kind of holy book—one that, if read properly, discloses the glory of God as eloquently as does the Koran itself.

Thinkers and Non-Thinkers

How, I wondered, is it that these entirely more nature-friendly aspects of the three religions of the Book are so little remarked upon today? Why, in particular, was it that the Christian thinkers who gave voice to the ancient cosmic vision of a nature every bit as worthy of rescue and redemption as humankind itself got so little attention in comparison to those for whom nature is at best a mere background to the human drama, and at worst the playground of the Devil?

To find out, I needed to go back to the Greek concept of multiple souls—in particular, to one of those souls called the *nous*. The *nous* was, according to Greek thinking, centered in the chest, and was responsible for thought, specifically *rational* thought. We are so at home with the notion that the brain is the seat of thinking that it is hard to imagine looking at it in any other way. But as we mentioned before, the brain was not always known as the thinking organ, and locating the origin of thought in the chest, and in particular the heart, was quite common in the ancient world. (This is an example of how hard it turns out to be to really place ourselves in the mind of a culture other than our own, for what we think about the world defines the way we experience it much more than we ordinarily realize.)

The really important thing about the *nous* for my investigations, however, was that animals were almost never said to possess it. In fact, the sole known reference to an animal possessing *nous* in Greek literature occurs in the *Odyssey*, when the dog Argus recognizes his master Odysseus after seventeen years away.

Plato was essentially a monotheist, and he sometimes described his Forms as living thoughts within the mind of God. This God-mind had a name as well. And as it turns out, Plato gave it the same name as the human rational capacity: *nous*. If humans have an immortal form, then, it must be their highest nature—their *nous*—joining with the *nous* of God.

So it was that I found myself at what turns out to be the very heart of the whole animals-don't-have-souls argument. For if the highest part of the soul is the rational part, and if heaven is itself a place of reason rather than emotion, it follows quite naturally that creatures that possessed no *nous* to speak of could not be expected to partake in the life that waits beyond the body.

Did this mean that the Platonic afterlife, abstract as it no doubt was, was also really a realm in which nature had no place at all? Plato never actually says this in his dialogues. But his pupil Aristotle very definitely *did* say it. If Plato was in large part an otherworldly mystic, Aristotle was his down-to-earth counterpart. *So* down-to-earth, in fact, that he had considerable doubts about whether the soul could exist apart from material creation at all. But, said Aristotle, if the soul *did* survive the death of the body, it was only the *nous*—the rational part—that did so. As the historian of ideas Richard Tarnas writes, "In Aristotle's view, the individual human soul might cease to exist with death, since the soul is vitally joined to the physical body it animates. The soul is the form of the body, just as the body is the matter of the soul. But the divine intellect, of which each man has a potential share and which distinguishes man from other animals, is immortal and transcendent. Indeed, man's highest happiness consists in the philosophical contemplation of eternal truth."

In other words, heaven, for Aristotle—if there *was* a heaven—

was made of thoughts. *Rational* thoughts. And for the ancients (who had never heard a pair of whales conversing or seen a chimp solve a logic puzzle or an African gray parrot chastise its owner in English for failing to feed it), rational thought was the domain of humans, and humans alone. So if any part of the human being actually *did* survive to enter this heaven, it would have to be the rational part as well. And this rational part was precisely the component of the soul that the later philosophers of Greece were least inclined to see animals as possessing.

The later Greeks were unashamedly in love with rational thought, and justifiably so, for if rationality is a key component of human thought, they developed that component to a degree unmatched by any culture before them, and we remain, today, hugely in their debt for doing so. But precisely because the things they discovered and accomplished by means of reason were so many and so great, this capacity eclipsed all other capacities of the mind (and spirit) in their estimation.

This enthusiasm for *ratio*, the capacity to uncover the workings of God through reason, was shared by many of the more influential Fathers of the Christian Church. In fact, Aristotle was the philosopher with the strongest single influence on mainstream Church philosophy for the first fifteen centuries of the Church's existence. And Aristotle's views on the irrational nature of the animal soul—and of nature in general—were very much a part of the Church's Greek intellectual inheritance.

It's a commonplace that one of the first things to get forgotten when Christian philosophers argue the subtleties of some recondite spiritual point is the clarity and directness with which Jesus himself always spoke. If Jesus' proclamations about animals are not plentiful (and if the episode of the Gadarene Swine always made me wonder if he had something against pigs), his general attitude toward them is more than clearly indicated in lines like "Look at the birds of the air, for they neither sow nor reap nor gather into barns; yet your heavenly Father feeds them," or "Are not five sparrows sold for two farthings, and not one of them is forgotten before God?"

It was words like these that inspired Saint Francis to address each animal he encountered as a fully individual being, every bit as deserving of his attention—and his conversation—as the human beings he interacted with. In fact, as I got more at home with the semi-hidden nature-loving side of Christianity, it occurred to me that Saint Francis bore a resemblance to a talented archaic shaman. Like the shaman, Francis seemed to have possessed a particularly strong ability to see the soul being—the animal-behind-the-animal—in every creature he met. Whether preaching to a flock of birds or chastising a wolf for chasing sheep, Francis clearly felt in his bones the truth proclaimed by the Gospel that each individual creature is really and truly present to God's eye.

Unfortunately, one reason Francis stands out in Christian history—and why for a long time he was the only animal-loving Christian I was even aware of—is that by the time of his birth in the twelfth century his spiritually inclusive attitude toward animals had become the exception rather than the rule. Despite the Gospels' clear and undeniable assertions that animals have a share in the redemption Christ held out to the world, memory of this faded away very quickly in the centuries that followed Christ's death on the cross. (Though at no single point did it ever die out completely, and in some sections of the Christian world, like Christian Ireland, animal-loving saints were seldom hard to find.)

Just a few scant centuries after the Gospels were written down, Saint Augustine stated that in heaven "there will be no animal body to 'weigh down the soul' in its process of corruption; there will be a spiritual body with no cravings, a body subdued in every part to the will." This "spiritual body" is the body that Saint Paul, in one of his many seed-and-agriculture-inspired passages, speaks of as having been "sown in corruption" and "raised in glory." But unlike Saint Paul, who, in spite of all his dogmatic thorniness on other issues, never seemed to deny animals and the rest of nature a place in the redeemed earth, Augustine is adamant that animals will *not* be present there. How could they be, when it is precisely the passionate, sub-rational aspects of our psyche that we share with the animals that we will most decisively leave behind when we enter the life of the world to come? "Because there is in man a rational soul," wrote Augustine in *The City of God*, "he subordinates to the peace of the rational soul all that part of his nature which he shares with the beasts." Human beings are, argued Augustine, the only creatures on earth blessed with the ability to think, and it's precisely this ability—in combination with God's grace—that allows us to survive death. This rational core is the part of us that God really cares about, and the sooner we can disentangle it from all those lower passions and desires that we share with the animals, the sooner we will be fit to enter into heaven—a heaven that will very definitely not be cluttered with any less-than-rational dogs, birds, or rabbits.

Different Kinds of Thinking,
Different Kinds of Thinkers

While fewer and fewer people in the modern world—and certainly precious few dog or cat owners—would subscribe to the idea that only human beings can think in any truly meaningful sense of the term, this idea was a surprisingly popular one for much of Western history. The idea that animals are essentially automatons reacting in a purely rote and mechanical matter to external stimuli has remained endemic to scientific thinking ever since René Descartes (who, oddly enough, had a dog of his own, of which he is said to have been very fond) brought it to the fore in the seventeenth century. Only in the latter half of the twentieth century did it become even remotely likely that a scientist studying animal behavior would see those animals through anything other than a purely mechanistic lens.

Students of animal behavior like Konrad Lorenz and contemporary writers on animal behavior like Marc Bekoff and Temple Grandin showed me that the key to appreciating animal thought is to accept it for what it is: *animal* rather than human. Like the hunter-gatherers who first studied and pondered the ways of animals millennia ago, the most perceptive modern students of animal behavior appreciate animals both for their commonalities with us and for their very real differences. All agree that the first step in respecting the workings of the animal mind is to stop demanding that it function exactly like a human mind.

This fact is made apparent to me every time I let Mercury, my Schipperke, out into the backyard of our Long Island house on his stationary extending leash. This leash goes just far enough for Mercury to make it around a tree that stands in the middle of the yard. Inevitably, Mercury will round this tree, start heading back to the house, and come to an abrupt and puzzled halt when the leash runs out of line. Looking at this dog of mine, whose personality I know so well and whose intelligence in other areas is so undeniable, standing there staring woefully back at the house completely stumped as to how to solve his predicament, I can understand how easy it would be for someone dead set against the idea that animals are thinking beings to leap on a moment like this as proof, pure and simple, that they aren't.

But they would be wrong to do so. For if Mercury lacks the gift of spatial abstraction that allows me to find his plight so ridiculous, it does not mean he doesn't possess the ability to experience himself and—even more important—communicate that experience of himself as an existentially situated being; a skill he demonstrates, loudly and pointedly, by barking at me to come help him out. Is Mercury acting mechanically when he does this? Not to my way of thinking. Mercury in these situations knows that he is in a fix, and that I can get him out of that fix, provided he can get my attention—just as I do when he is having one of the bad dreams to which, as he ages, he seems ever more susceptible. Though not a rational creature on the level that (at my better moments at least) I am, Mercury is a *thinking being,* and for me to see him as anything else would be to blind myself to the evidence he presents to me each day as my companion and friend.

The Ladder of Being

The literature on the shape and nature of animal intelligence—what it is, what it isn't, and how it differs from the human variety—is massive. But to understand the basic idea that the animal mind can be honored without equating it completely with that of humans, we need only summon up the key idea that lay behind the primordial mapping of the multilevel universe traversed by the spirits of humans, gods, and animals: the concept of hierarchy.

The word *hierarchy* sounds bossy and constrictive to modern ears, but in its original meaning (*hiero* + *arche*, or "holy structure"), it had much more to do with matters of spirit than with matters of power. (It's very hard, unless one is an absolutely rigid materialist, *not* to take a hierarchical view of the world, and even such committed cosmic democrats as the Taoists, through their distinction between the phenomenal and spiritual levels of reality, betrayed themselves as hierarchical thinkers as well.) While the notion that the universe is a wedding-cake-like structure leading from the material up to the spiritual was, as we saw earlier, pioneered by primordial humanity, the version of this idea that has been most influential in Western thought is the Great Chain of Being, which comes to us from the Greeks. This version, if we examine it with the right attitude, allows us to see animals as thinking (and hence heaven-worthy) beings without claiming that their intelligence is equal or identical to ours.

At the bottom of the Great Chain is inert matter—the most obvious natural example of which is a rock. Rocks don't move, and (if we leave out the tricky issue of crystals) they don't grow. Basically, they just sit there. Above (and with that word we have, of course, already entered into hierarchical thinking) the world of inert matter we have plants. Plants are plainly alive. They grow, and if we watch certain species closely we can see that they move, too—if generally much more slowly than people or animals do. We could, then, say that plants are

Matter + Life.

Above plants, we get to the world of animals. Animals possess life the way plants do, but they also possess something more: a "something" that allows them to move around, make decisions, and take an active, conscious part in the world that is clearly a step above the part that plants take. (Whether or not insects and other lower animals can be said to do such things is a matter of much argument, but for our purposes we don't need to get caught up in it. Suffice it to say that there is a general movement *upward* in the categories of existing things, with countless possible sub-gradations that could be added if we take the entire animate world into account.)

Using an equation again, we could say that animals are

Matter + Life + Consciousness.

Moving a rung further up, we get to humans. Once again according to the traditional Greek scheme, humans have a certain something-more-ness to them as well: one that all the levels beneath them lack. Like rocks, we humans possess matter (our bodies). Like plants, we possess life (that mysterious, invisible "something" that leaves at death, when our bodies transform from animated objects into lumps of inert matter). And like animals, we possess a mind that allows us to make decisions—

to live and move actively upon the earth rather than statically and passively the way plants generally do. But . . . we also have something else: a something-else that is traditionally defined as self-awareness. Humans, this line of argument goes, not only think—we *know* that we think.

As the economist and philosopher E. F. Schumacher points out, these four basic levels of being are increasingly rare the farther up the scale one goes. "Matter," he writes, "cannot be destroyed. Compared with inanimate matter, life is rare and precarious; in turn, compared with the ubiquitousness and tenacity of life, consciousness is even rarer and more vulnerable. Self-awareness is the rarest power of all, precious and vulnerable to the highest degree, the supreme and generally fleeting achievement of a person, present one moment and all too easily gone the next."

And beyond humans? This, not surprisingly, was the point where the classical philosophers started to argue. *Was* there anything above humans, or did the ladder of creation come to a halt with them? According to traditional Christian thought (and the more esoteric branches of Islamic and Hebrew thought as well), the Great Chain had *many* links in it above humans: ones that were every bit as real as those below, even if they were largely invisible to ordinary sight. Each of these different levels was associated, as in ancient Greek thought, with a particular star or planet, and with the specific variety of spiritual being (gods for the Greeks, angels for the Christians) that was in charge of it. According to this hierarchical vision (which held sway right up to the advent of modern science, which abruptly dismantled it in the late sixteenth century), the universe was a house of many floors: one in which every object, every animal, every human being, and every angel declared in every aspect of its being the level to which it belonged. And because the house itself was good (how could it not be if it was made by God?) each being that dwelled within it possessed an essential soundness and goodness, too (which is why Aquinas, following Aristotle, could celebrate the essential goodness and integrity of animal creation, even if he denied it a place in heaven).

Seen in this light, the concept of hierarchy becomes a strangely generous, strangely *democratic* idea. Though easily given to perversion and misrepresentation, in its more benign and sophisticated versions the Great Chain is arguably the single most important and enduring idea about the basic nature of the cosmos in the history of human thought.

Though the idea of the cosmos as a spiritual hierarchy was born in the Stone Age, primitive humanity didn't understand it in quite the same way that the full-fledged philosophers who took it over from them later did. To begin with, the primordial model of the Great Chain doesn't have quite the tidiness that the later philosophical versions of it do. Stones, for example, were never seen as purely inert objects by primitive peoples (as the anthropologist Tylor knew very well when he coined the term *animism*). A stone was not only alive, it was also—to a degree at least—conscious, and a stone (either a natural one or a carved statue) that held a particular spirit could be *highly* conscious. Plants, too, according to the primitive model, were both alive and conscious as well. Plants knew things and, according to the views of many primitive peoples, had guardian spirits from whom important knowledge—such as whether a particular plant was safe to eat or not or whether it was otherwise of use to humans—could be gleaned.

But all these differences are, in the end, unimportant. What matters most about the Great Chain is not how one goes about dividing up the levels within it, but that one sees those levels as *unified* with one another, all sharing membership in a cosmos that is ordered, unified, and permeated by intelligence from the top (God or the Divine or the Origin or whatever name one chooses) all the way on down to the material level. (For even unthinking matter manifests, in its molecular and submolecular structure, the irreducibly intelligent nature of all creation.)

That sense of the universe's all-pervasive intelligence is, in the end, the greatest single gift that the concept of the Great Chain gives us, for it allows us to look at all beings as *manifesting* intelligence and divinity, without necessarily being in conscious charge of that intelligence to the degree that we humans are. A common house mouse carries all the mystery and brilliance of creation within it, but it is not *aware* of this fact in the way that, say, Plato was. For me to look at my dog Mercury as my complete equal would be, to my mind, foolish, for even when he's not staring at me from the end of a tangled leash, I know that I am in possession of a mind that is capable not only of comprehending more of the world than his is, but that I am also *conscious* of the *fact* that I am. But just because I acknowledge this fact doesn't mean I need to write him off as an insignificant being. That's the magic of the Great Chain: it allows me to embrace other beings without pretending to make myself one hundred percent equal to them in all respects. When I look at Mercury, straining hopelessly at his leash and barking for me to come let him loose, with the older, kinder versions of the Great Chain in mind, what I see is a being who is different from me, in some ways even perhaps inferior to me, but who is nonetheless part and parcel of the same multilevel universe that I am. By virtue of that common membership, it really doesn't matter how much or how little intelligence we share, or how different his style of intelligence may be from mine. The very fact that we both live as members in good standing of that great multi-storied cosmic house seals our essential kinship.

A Break in the Ladder

But with Aristotle and his doctrine of the *nous*—and in particular his claim that humans possess it while animals don't—a barricade seems suddenly to rise up at the midsection of the Great Chain. With the birth of the Aristotelian view of the cosmos, and the adoption of that view by the dominant fathers of the Christian church, animals lost all connection to the higher levels of the Great Chain. Though created by an intelligent God, they were not participants in that intelligence, but only passing manifestations of it. Rational thought, plucked from the complex matrix of qualities and abilities that makes us who and what we are, became equated with all that was uniquely valuable about humankind. And because spiritual survival demanded the ability to consciously exercise such rational thought, animals lost all hope of any place in any heaven or afterlife worthy of the name.

Ratio—the Latin root from which the word *rational* derives—was, for both Augustine and Aquinas, the equivalent of the Greek *nous*. Like the nose of a rocketship that penetrates the heavens after all of its lower sections have fallen away, it was *ratio*, and *ratio* alone, that made it into the spiritual regions stretching above the earth. Animals, like the rest of nature, were, to the Aristotelian mind, incapable not just of the rationality that humans are, but of any kind of genuine thought or consciousness whatsoever. And because they were, no heaven worthy of the name could grant them entry.

Once animals had been our spiritual peers who descended with us from the world above, and were on their way back to that world as well. Among the ancient Near Eastern agricultural cities they were spiritually charged beings who did not entirely lose that status despite the fact that they could also be owned, traded, used, and sacrificed as property. In the Christian era, animals suffered a further demotion. They now were little more than things: objects that we could use and abuse as we wished while stuck down here on the material level, but that we needn't worry about running into when we left this world behind for heaven. With the denial of any kind of genuine mental life to animals, and by that association any kind of genuine soul life either, it was really only a step or two to the nightmare world of Cartesian science. The father of all the mechanistic conceptions of nature that we are so familiar with today, Descartes, his own pet dog aside, was convinced that animals were not even *matter-plus-life-plus-consciousness*, but simply *matter-plus-life*. So convinced was Descartes that animals were in essence unconscious robots that he would nail other living dogs to planks of wood in order that their struggles wouldn't get in the way while he dissected them alive.

Before the fall, according to the primordial view, humans

and animals were both soul-beings who took the plunge into incarnate existence together and would, by hook or by crook, return to the world of spirit together as well. At the dawn of the Christian era, many voices within that tradition (joined soon thereafter by voices in the Judaic and Islamic traditions as well) made that same argument. But in the ensuing centuries that view was doomed to be the minority one, thanks to the power of the idea that heaven was, above all else, a rational place, and that humans, as the earth's sole rational animals, would alone be admitted. The original mystery that defined our relationship with animals for eons had been replaced by a cold and unfeeling mastery.

Was this really the best that we humans could do for the fellow creatures that had not only accompanied us on our journey out of nature and into culture, but without whom that journey would never have been possible? I, of course, didn't think so.

Nor, it turned out, was I the only citizen of the modern world who felt that way. Not by a long shot.

The Bridge

It must be restated that there remains a distinction between the soul of an animal and that of man. According to Scripture the animal is destined to perish. It is mortal by definition, unlike man who continues his existence beyond earthly life. So far as we understand now there is no possibility that we will find other creatures in the Hereafter. However, it's one thing to expound according to the theology and philosophy we have studied and quite another for us to comprehend Divine reality—both future and distant—which remains mysterious and difficult to grasp within our limited capabilities.

—Theologian Carlo Molari, commenting on a controversial remark by Pope John Paul II that animals have been given the "breath of life" just as humans have

All creatures are balanced upon the creative word of God, as if upon a bridge of diamond.

—Philaret of Moscow (1782–1867)

A Manatee Named Moose

In 1993, while in the midst of my researches for that coffee-table book on the monkey in art, I moved from San Diego to New York. Not too long after that book was done, I got a contract to write a memoir about growing up with my father, in particular that stretch of the 1970s during which *The Secret Life of Plants* had made him momentarily famous. My animal-soul researches faded out for a while.

Then, in 1999, after five years of struggling along in New York without a full-time job, I took an editorial position at a magazine called *Guideposts*. Started in 1949 by Norman Vincent Peale, the magazine was based on Peale's quirky but popular melding of old-fashioned, all-American, can-do optimism with Christianity. Most of the stories in *Guideposts*—which my new job required me to assemble and edit—turned in one way or another around the idea that with God's help and the right attitude, there is no obstacle in life that can't be overcome.

Most issues of *Guideposts* have at least one animal story in them, and these soon became my favorites to work on. Dog or cat stories were fun, but the best featured wild animals. These latter stories, however, often came with problems attached. *Guideposts* stories are often based on taped interviews, the editor's job being to shape the spoken narrative into a short, readable story with what the editors call a "take-away" at the end—a positive message that will linger in the reader's mind after the magazine has been put down. The general mandate at *Guideposts* was that all stories were to have a positive take-away, but finding them for wild-animal stories wasn't always easy. These stories often ended with a sad event: the animal died, or disappeared, or something else went wrong to disrupt all the fun, happy stuff that went on at the beginning.

"This has been in inventory for a while," my supervisor Rick said one day, handing me a folder with the word *Moose*, written across it in pen. "Maybe you can do something with it."

The story was narrated by a veterinarian at Sea World Orlando named Deke Beusse and was not, as the word scribbled on the folder had instantly led me to suspect, about an actual moose, but about Deke's relationship with a young Florida manatee that went by that name:

> In 1991, a call came in from some folks in the Daytona area about an orphaned manatee swimming aimlessly in a residential canal. When we got there we saw that he was just a baby—so young that his umbilical cord still trailed behind him. But he was already big: about four-and-a-half feet long and close to 100 pounds. We christened him "Moose."
>
> Moose settled right in at Sea World. He made friends with the other manatees, and charmed all us humans too. Manatees are friendly by nature, but Moose took to people like no other I'd seen. As soon as he noticed someone approaching his pool, he'd swim over and put his pectoral flippers up on the side, squeaking until he got a scratch on the head or belly.
>
> Moose quickly graduated from a baby bottle to a diet of solid food. Soon he was packing away all the spinach and romaine lettuce we could give him. In 1993, when the public manatee pool opened, Moose became its star. The manatees of the world couldn't have asked for a better representative.

The story did not, however, end there.

By the summer of 1995, Moose was nine feet long and close to 1,000 pounds. Sea World's policy is to release all its manatees once they are fully rehabilitated. As tough as it was to say good-bye, the time came for us to send Moose back into the wild.

For a few weeks, we kept track of Moose through a temporary radio transmitter we'd attached to his tail. He was getting around and appeared to be adapting well to life outside Sea World.

Then, some six months after the release, a call came in from the Department of Environmental Protection reporting an unusually large dead manatee in a canal. It was Moose. Lacerations on his hide showed he had been struck by the propeller of a speeding powerboat.

I decided Deke's story was too likable not to make it into the magazine, and set to work squeezing enough of a positive message out of it (though Moose was dead, the work to save other manatees went on, etc.) to make it qualify, at least technically, as an uplifting story. Yet just beneath the surface, it remained what it had been when it came in: a very sad story about a friendship between a human and an animal that had ended in death.

Happy-Sad

I ended up working on a number of these pretend-happy animal stories at *Guideposts*, enough to notice certain regularities in them. These regularities were not just in the stories themselves, but also in my emotional reaction to them as I put them together.

What really caught my attention was the fact that though these stories always made me sad, they never made me *just* sad. Instead, the main feeling I got as I worked on them was sadness mixed with another, more mysterious feeling: one that was so strong sometimes, it was almost physical. A feeling that, if I had to name it, I guess I would call hope.

Guideposts didn't introduce me to this feeling. I'd experienced it many times over the years, mostly when I was very young. I first remembered getting it when my mother read certain stories to me. The ending of *Charlotte's Web*, for example—when Charlotte dies but leaves her brood of babies to keep Wilbur the pig company after she's gone—gave it to me. Later on, in my early teens, reading the animal stories of Ernest Thompson Seton and the nature essays of Loren Eiseley, and books like *That Quail Robert* and *A Seal Called Andre*, I got it again. It was a weird, almost convulsive feeling of sadness—as if something immeasurably huge and important had been lost—combined with a small but powerful feeling of hope: hope that whatever that huge, lost thing was, it wasn't really gone for good.

I also got this feeling from movies. The ending of *The Yearling* produced it, as did the scene in Mike Nichols's film *The Day of the Dolphin* when George C. Scott's character is forced to send the two dolphins he has trained to speak English back into the wild. In order to end the bond he has created with them, Scott's character has to tell the dolphins he is not their friend, and for me the line "Pa no love Fa" carried with it a weight of such sadness that it all but completely blotted out the small hint of hope and happiness that the film somehow still managed to leave me with.

By the time I saw *The Day of the Dolphin* in the early seventies, I had come up with a simple yet accurate name for this feeling. I called it Happy-Sad.

A year or so after putting together Deke's story, a book came across my desk by a man named Jack Becklund. *Summers with the Bears* was about a stretch of years that Jack and his wife, Patti, spent in a house in the Minnesota woods, and the black bears they had made friends with while there. One bear in particular—a cub that ambled up their driveway one afternoon during their first spring in the house—was the focus of the story.

Jack was the first to see her, and was none too happy about it, as he and Patti had been spending weeks trying to discourage the large local bear population from snooping around their house. "Oh, he's just a poor little orphan," Patti said as the cub set to work on the sunflower seeds in the Becklunds' bird feeder. The Becklunds christened the cub—which turned out to be a female—Little Bit, and over the following months and years, she became one of those remarkable dual creatures that one so often reads about in animal books: one that, while completely retaining her membership in the wild world out beyond the human community, becomes an honorary member of the human world as well. Through Little Bit, the Becklunds got a taste of that old, paradisiacal world where humans and animals, though different, lived under a single roof.

Though Jack and Patti often worried about whether they were being a good influence on Little Bit, she eventually grew into a fully competent wild bear right before their eyes. In her third year with the Becklunds, Little Bit came out of her winter hibernation with two cubs. They were rebellious, and initially more than Little Bit could handle. But two years later, when Little Bit came to the Becklund's backyard with a new set of cubs, they were model children in every respect.

Each September, when bear-hunting season rolled around, the Becklunds went through agonies wondering if Little Bit would escape the guns of the local hunters while out in the woods. Late one summer, in addition to the impending gunfire, the Becklunds got something else to worry about. Patti's dad out in California was diagnosed with cancer.

Just a few weeks after the diagnosis, he passed away. "When the phone call came with news of his death," Jack writes, "I had just gone for a walk down the driveway with our dog Sheba. So Patti stepped out on the deck where Little Bit was sitting and nestled herself beside the huge bundle of fur.

"When I walked into the living room, I spied Patti outside. I went out and sat down. Her arms encircled the bear's neck and she was sobbing with her eyes closed.

" 'What is it?' I asked quietly.

" 'Dad died.' Her words were muffled into Little Bit's fur coat. 'I just got the call.' She sat quietly with the bear for another half minute, then Little Bit leaned her massive head against Patti's. I knew she understood nothing of what was going on, but she felt something and responded. It was a magic moment in a time of grief and one I will never forget."

A little later that same September, Jack looked out one afternoon to see Little Bit sitting on the back deck, her nose and paws covered with rust-colored dirt.

" 'Getting ready, eh?' I said, bringing out a small handful of nuts for her to munch. This was the only nourishment we had seen her take for over a week.

"She and Winnie and Pooh [her latest pair of cubs] stayed on the back deck for a couple of hours. We went to sit with them until they left. In late afternoon, Little Bit got up, went down the steps and started across the lawn. Pooh stayed close by her mother, while Winnie brought up the rear. As she reached the creek, Little Bit stopped to wait for Winnie and turned to look back for just a moment. Patti whispered, 'Go with the Lord, Little Bit.' Then Little Bit led the cubs across the creek's rocky bottom and up into the shady woods. We heard them a few seconds longer. Then they were gone."

That turned out to be the last that Jack and Patti would see of Little Bit. Whether she succumbed to a hunter or perished in hibernation during the winter, the following spring saw the return of other bears they had become familiar with, but no Little Bit. Their time with her was over.

Condensing Jack and Patti's story for the magazine, I struggled through all the familiar problems that tales like theirs always brought up. Black bears, my boss pointed out, were lovable. But they were also large, powerful, potentially dangerous animals, and by publishing a story that treated them like a bunch of backyard songbirds, I was placing the magazine at risk. What if a reader, following the Becklunds' actions, got himself or herself injured by a bear?

"Bears," he said, summing up his reservations, "aren't pets."

And of course they weren't. Black bears are considerably smaller and milder than the giant bears of prehistory that so terrified and inspired primitive humanity, but they are bears all the same. The *New Oxford American Dictionary* definition of "pet" is "a domestic or tamed animal or bird kept for companionship or pleasure and treated with care and affection," and "domestic" derives from the Latin *domus*: house. In coaxing Little Bit to the edge of her and Jack's house, Patti was indeed making a pet of sorts of the bear. But rather than diminishing Little Bit's status in doing so, she was, it seemed to me, expanding the whole concept of what a pet really is. All pets descend from wild animals. As such, the most thoroughly domesticated of them remains a messenger from a place apart: a place that is increasingly hard to stay in touch with in the modern world, and a place that, more than ever, we rely on them to keep in contact with.

Little Bit, in sitting next to Patti and resting her massive head on her shoulder, was demonstrating what animals, whether domestic, wild, or somewhere in between, when treated with care and affection, have always demonstrated to humans over the course of our dual histories: they need us. Not for food, not for protection (though of course for the domestic and some of the wild ones these come in handy), but because there is something in us that draws animals to us. Just as they give us a piece of the old paradise that we no longer quite have, we impart, through our humanity, a piece of that paradise that they in turn are missing. In the original days of spirit before the fall into the world we know today, animals and humans were both different from the way they are now. To state it a little too simply (but accurately nonetheless), animals were more *human*, which is why the myths of so many primitive peoples talk about animals becoming more humanlike when they reenter the spirit world. And humans in turn were, in that distant age, more animal-like, in that we possessed an innocence that the earthly journey into culture has brought us ever further from.

Patti had chosen Little Bit's name well, for just as we offer a little bit of the old paradise to animals, so animals, in turn, make available a little bit of it to us.

The Step-Out Moment

Summers with the Bears is illustrated with a number of photos of Little Bit and the other bears the Becklunds befriended—along with a mixed bag of other, less imposing forest visitors like squirrels and chipmunks—hanging out in Patti and Jack's backyard. In one of the most affecting, Patti and Little Bit sit side by side on the edge of the porch. Little Bit is hanging her front paws over the railing and inclining her head slightly toward Patti, as if listening carefully to something she is saying.

This photo put me in mind of a particular kind of photo or video clip that would regularly get forwarded to me on my *Guideposts* e-mail address. These photos featured a particular kind of interaction between animals and humans, or between animals and other animals: one in which the animal in question steps out of character, becoming for a moment a different *kind* of animal than it normally is.

The Internet is full of video clips featuring such moments. As I write this, the one making the rounds features a lion named Christian. As a cub, the clip tells us, Christian was purchased by two men who saw him for sale in a London department store. A

pastor friend of theirs allowed Christian the run of the grounds of his church. Christian grew, and eventually the men decided that even with all that grass to run on, he would be better off in the wild. So they returned him to Africa and set him free. A year later they returned to pay him a visit. The Internet clip shows what happened when they did. Christian sees his former owners, runs toward them, leaps up, and—in an extraordinarily affectionate and strangely human way—embraces them. He even brings his mate, a wild lioness, to meet his human friends and she allows them to pet her.

Step-out moments between animals (quite often between a predator and a prey species) are equally popular. A few months back, for example, several people sent me a photo of a group of huskies frolicking on the Arctic ice with a polar bear. Large, presumably ferocious animals like lions and bears are especially attractive step-out moment subjects. (The photo of Patti and Little Bit, Jack writes, was published in the Becklunds' local paper and drew a large and overwhelmingly positive response.) This is, I suspect, because they speak directly to our frustrations at the world as we know it, and to our half-concealed paradisiacal nostalgia for the very different world we dimly remember its once being. In the world we know today, lions kill and eat other animals. Christian, we can assume, was not living as a vegetarian out there on the African plains before his adoptive human parents came to visit, but spent his time chasing after gazelle and antelope (or waiting around for his mate to do so for him). What we see in the clip is not this game-eating predator, however, but a very different being: one whose behavior harks back to the time of paradise, when all

creatures lived unburdened by strife and violence, by the need to eat and the danger of being eaten.

Is our love of such step-out moments anthropomorphizing, or somehow disrespectful to the true wild identities of the creatures that show up in them? I don't think so—any more than are the myths and tales of primitive peoples that describe animals behaving in distinctly human ways. The aspect of the animals in these moments that steps out into view is not the animal's falsely imagined human identity, but its very real, if usually hidden, spiritual one. It was precisely this spiritual core that Jack and Patti's warm and democratic attitude to the animals in their backyard brought out—both in the animals and in themselves.

"Nothing Gold Can Stay"

"These are golden days," Jack had written in his journal one summer day when Little Bit and her friends were out behind the Becklunds' house and all was well with the world. "Golden," I thought—with its overtones of joy tinged with impending loss—was just the right word for him to have used. "Nothing gold can stay," Robert Frost famously wrote, and I think about that line whenever I read a story of a human-animal friendship like the one between Jack and Patti and Little Bit: a story that reminded me that though humans and animals belong "under one roof," in this world they can rarely stay that way.

According to the Makiritare people of Venezuela's Orinoco Valley, human beings were on the verge of being born from a giant egg when Odosha—the Makiritare equivalent of the Devil—let night escape into the world from a medicine pouch.

Odosha, writes the historian of religions Lawrence Sullivan, "governs this world with sickness, death, and the darkness of night." But he will not do so forever. For there is another egg, hidden away within Mount Waruma Hidi, the Makiritare's cosmic mountain. Within this egg there lives a people untouched by the evil and darkness of this present world. Quoting from *Watunna*, the creation cycle of the Makiritare people, Sullivan writes that if one listens carefully one can hear the laughter and singing of this good people, hidden away deep within their egg.

Those people, the Makiritare believe, are not destined to stay inside that egg forever. As the creator god Wanadi himself explained to the Makiritare before his departure from the present world, another, better world will one day come into being. Long ago, at a feast where all the "grandfathers" of today's humanity were gathered, Wanadi explained that he could no longer remain with them in the world as it had now become. "I'm going," Wanadi told the grandfathers. But he would be back in the future, when the Devil Odosha was gone.

"When Odosha dies, the Earth will end. Then there will be another one, a good one. The sun, the moon, the stars are all going to fall on the Earth. This sky is going to fall. It's a bad sky, a fake one. Then you'll see the good sky (heaven) again, the real one, like in the beginning. When the sun falls, Wanadi's light will come back and shine. I'll return. I'll send you my new *damodede* [spirit double], the new Wanadi. It will be me with another body, the Wanadi of the new Earth. I'll go find *Heuhanna* [the stone egg with the good people inside] in the mountain. The unborn people are waiting for me to be born."

Male and female, human and animal, matter and spirit—

everything in the world as we know it is defined by separation. But that state of separation, say the spiritual traditions of the world with virtually one voice, did not always exist. In the days before the Fall, life—both for humans and for animals—had been defined by unity rather than by separation, and so it would be again someday. Both animal and human will recover those missing aspects of themselves that, in the fragmentation wrought by the Fall, no longer allowed creatures from different levels of the chain of being to commune directly and easily with one another. So said the myths of the primordial hunter-gatherers. So, too, in different ways, said the myths of the planting peoples, and of the city-builders that came after them. And so said the great world religions as well—not all the time, but here and there, in voices that were quieter, less insistent and obtrusive, but perhaps for those very reasons more convincing than the other, more-strident voices of those traditions that spoke to the contrary. No matter what else was going on in the world, that old, original story of the loss and recovery of the unity and accord of all creation was always being told by someone, somewhere.

At one point during my days of working on Deke Beusse's manatee story, my boss raised a question. "What," he asked, "is the manatee in this piece?"

"What do you mean?" I asked.

"I mean," he said, "what does he stand for in terms of the story's narrative?"

I cast about for a moment, then said playfully, "The manatee is a Christ figure."

My response got the predicted laughter. But the fact is,

beneath the surface I was being perfectly serious. Standing in a crowded peasants' festival before a mounted calf's head, the early twentieth-century Austrian poet Georg Trakl famously muttered, "That is our Lord Christ." I've always loved that remark, and have noticed that when the people—scholars, psychologists, literary critics—who write about Trakl bring this incident up, it is usually in order to cite it as evidence of Trakl's unbalanced character. After all, who in their right mind would see the face of Jesus in the severed head of a calf?

But as my years at *Guideposts* passed, I came to see that remark of Trakl's as not so much crazy as prophetic. Trakl was a profoundly troubled soul, but he was also a genuine visionary, and I found his strange outburst just as compelling as the much more famous incident in which the philosopher Friedrich Nietzsche broke down at the Piazza Carlo Alberto in Italy a decade and a half earlier. Seeing a horse being whipped, Nietzsche had thrown his arms around the suffering animal, and then collapsed into a state of madness (brought on in part by a venereal disease he had contracted) from which he never recovered.

Both of these anecdotes, eccentric and vaguely apocryphal as they sound, carry to my mind an undeniable significance in light of the story of the animal soul through history. Not simply because an important philosopher and a celebrated poet were moved by the plight of an animal, but because for a single agonizing moment that plight revealed to them the terrible off-kilter-ness of the world—an off-kilter-ness of which all beings on earth, both human and animal, suffer the results.

The Pearly Gates

The more time I spent at *Guideposts*, the more interested I got in trying to figure out what kind of stories might appeal to the magazine's readers. As I was not exactly the average *Guideposts* reader myself (my spiritual inclinations tending, as they do, to the quirky and recondite), this was often somewhat challenging. The easiest place of overlap—especially in light of my desire to reconcile Christianity with a genuine respect for nature—lay with animals. Was there, I wondered, an animal angle that had never been covered in the magazine before that I might get some enjoyment from working on?

One day at work I stumbled on a Web reference to a book by a woman named M. Jean Holmes called *Do Dogs Go to Heaven?* I asked Sharon, one of the administrative assistants at the office who also does a truly heroic amount of animal-rescue work, to see if she could get in touch with Mrs. Holmes. A week later, Sharon came into my office with the book. "I talked to her on the phone," Sharon said. "She's nice, and I could tell she's a real animal person. She put this right in the mail for us." On the book's cover was a painting of Saint Peter standing at the gates of Heaven studying his famous scroll. Arranged on the clouds before him was an array of animals: a German shepherd, a dachshund, several cats, a pig, a parrot . . . and a rabbit. Inside, the book was inscribed by the author, along with the words "The Lord says Yes!"

I started reading. Jean opened her book with a description of a quest her mother, Irene, had begun when she was in her seventies following the death of her chocolate-point dachshund, Choc.

Sometime after Choc died, Jean and her mother were chatting with a part-time preacher who also delivered their newspaper.

"He was not well educated [wrote Jean], but he was a hard-working fellow who appeared to love the Lord. Suddenly Mom asked this preacher:

'Do dogs go to heaven?'

"Instantly, I was curious as to how the preacher would answer. He looked surprised. He paused and thought. Then he said, 'Well, in the Book of Revelation, it says that Jesus is coming back on a horse. So there are horses in heaven.' He paused and thought some more.

"From the look on his face, it was obvious he was searching his mind for Bible verses. 'It also says, "without the gates are the dogs." So, dogs aren't in heaven.'

"The preacher didn't know that the term 'dog' in that passage is a slang expression [for nonbelievers]. I knew, but remained quiet."

Jean's mother, however, *didn't* remain quiet. Over the next few weeks she asked every local pastor she could find that same question. She got a different answer every time—most of them negative, all of them confusing. "The more Mom asked her question," Jean wrote, "the more my amusement died. It occurred to me that I had never, in all my years of church attendance, ever heard a sermon on animals going to heaven."

The rest of Jean's book was an attempt, largely using scriptural references that those country preachers her mom questioned had somehow overlooked, to answer the question "Do pets go to heaven?" more satisfactorily. After reading Jean's book I did some more research and discovered that in the years since Angus had died and I'd done most of my investigations into the animal soul, there had been a curious bump in books on the topic. Most of these had come out in the early nineties, right around the time my own reading on the subject had slacked off, and most were written from a Christian perspective.

I ordered a bunch of these books, and read them. A surprising number of the authors began their discussions with stories very similar to that of Jean's about her mom. After the death of a beloved pet, he or she had sought solace with a pastor, only to be given a confused—and confusing—reply about the postmortem fate of their pet, or, worse, to be told straight out that their pet was gone forever.

None of the stories in these books particularly surprised me. I knew well enough by that point that our twin cultural legacies of religion and science were *both* adamant that the notion of an animal's soul surviving death was preposterous. Standing at the gates of the rational Heaven that had appeared so early on in Christian history, Aristotle still blocked the way of animals through the Pearly Gates—even though most people, and a good chunk of pastors, most likely had no idea of the history of the ideas that formed the grounds of their disbelief.

Brenda

Every day when I walked out the doors of the *Guideposts* offices on 34th Street, I would leave the world of the magazine's readers behind and step into the crowded, fast-moving stream of savvy, secular New York. Not that New York was really all that secular, as the plentiful shingles and shop windows for fortune-tellers, new age bookstores, and start-up yoga studios I passed on the way home would remind me.

One day on this homeward walk I ran into a woman named Brenda who lived in my apartment building. Brenda worked in the fashion industry, and lately I'd begun to see her on my morning dog walk coming back to the building with a yoga mat under her arm. Thin, blond, and always well dressed—even on her way back from exercising—she struck me as the quintessential embodiment of modern, urban, post-Christian spirituality. Though I didn't know anything about the specifics of her beliefs, I could only assume that they were Eastern—either Buddhist or Hindu—and about as far from the religious views of the average reader of *Guideposts* as it was possible to get.

We walked the remaining blocks to our building together. Brenda asked me how my day had been, and—remembering how distraught she had been after losing her dog Cosmo a few years back—I decided to lay out for her what I'd been thinking about recently: writing an article for the magazine on whether animals have souls.

"Wow," said Brenda. "That reminds me of a story."

Brenda told me she'd grown up in L.A., in a section of the Hollywood Hills that was still fairly wild. "When I was in third grade," she told me, "my girlfriend Dominique's cat had kittens. I pleaded with my mom and dad to let me have one. I picked the smallest one in the litter—a tabby. My dad named her Poquito, which means 'Little One' in Spanish, but I just called her Punky. My mom and dad got divorced a couple of years later, and Punky was my living security blanket. Whatever went on during the day, I knew I could always count on her being down at the foot of my bed at night."

Brenda was in seventh grade when Punky went out one night and didn't come back. "I was totally heartbroken," Brenda said. "I went to a Lutheran private school, and in religion class one day after Punky disappeared, Mr. Toback gave us a true-false test. One of the questions was 'Do animals have souls?' I marked it 'true.'

"When Mr. Toback gave us our quizzes back, there was a big 'X' next to the question about animals having souls. I raised my hand. 'Why is this marked wrong?' I asked. I really thought he must have made a mistake."

He hadn't.

" 'Brenda,' Mr. Toback said, 'animals don't have souls and they don't go to heaven.' Those words kicked loose a whole avalanche of thoughts in my head—thoughts I'd never realized I had about religion, about whether any of it was really true or not. As a kid there are a bunch of things that you just kind of *know* are true. You don't need anyone to tell you they are because they're obvious. Or at least so I'd thought up till then.

"Walking home that day, I couldn't get Mr. Toback's words— and that image of a heaven full of people and no animals—out of my head. It wasn't the first time an adult had told me something I disagreed with. But it was the first time I remember getting this feeling inside that I just knew it was *wrong*. My thinking on religion changed that day. In fact, that was the day my real spiritual journey began. If being a Lutheran meant going to a heaven with a bunch of people in it and no animals, then I wasn't interested.

I think that experience was what led me to my interest in other religions. It was a negative experience, but it had a positive effect, I guess, in that it made me the person I am today."

The Rainbow Bridge

Brenda may have been, in most respects, very different from most of the readers of *Guideposts*, but with her determination to answer "yes" to the question of whether or not animals have souls, she was just like them. Just as I was like them, too. There was, to me, something kind of surprising and wonderful about this commonality. When a bunch of people who are very different in other ways feel strongly about an issue, it usually means there's some validity to what they think. It was time, I decided, that the Mr. Tobacks of the world heard more from people like Brenda, Jean, and me. My time of silent pondering about the question of whether animals have souls or not was over, and my time of writing about it was beginning.

The day after that walk with Brenda, I went to my boss and told him I wanted to put together a piece on the subject of pets and the afterlife.

"Why not?" he said. "No one's ever done that in the magazine before."

The article came out in the February 2005 issue under the title "Will My Pet Go to Heaven?" I decided to focus the piece on the Hebrew term *nephesh* and how the true meaning of that word had been glossed over by many of the Bible's commentators and translators. I quoted Isaiah's prophetic passage about a time to come when the lion would lie down with the lamb, and talked a little bit about the rainbow that God sets in the sky after the flood in Genesis, as a promise that the link between the divine and the earthly will never again be broken. Leaving out the complexities of the Hebrew view of the human soul, the Hebrew and Christian relationship to Greek thought, and other such thorny matters, my conclusion was a simple but heartfelt one: not only does the Bible in both the Hebrew and New Testaments provide plenty of suggestions that animals are valuable before God, but the evidence of our hearts does so as well. Augustine and Aquinas (I mentioned them briefly too) might disagree, but from my perspective, any heaven that didn't include animals would clearly be less than truly heavenly.

I also mentioned, in passing, a popular piece that had circulated on the Internet called "The Rainbow Bridge." The poem talked about a bridge that the souls of the dead cross when they come to heaven, and the pets that they find waiting for them on it:

Just this side of heaven is a place called Rainbow Bridge.
When an animal dies that has been especially close to someone here, that pet goes to Rainbow Bridge.
There are meadows and hills for all of our special friends so they can run and play together.
There is plenty of food, water and sunshine, and our friends are warm and comfortable.
All the animals who had been ill and old are restored to health and vigor; those who were hurt or maimed are made whole and strong again, just as we remember them in our dreams of days and times gone by.

The animals are happy and content, except for one small thing;
they each miss someone very special to them, who had to be
left behind.

They all run and play together, but the day comes when one
suddenly stops and looks into the distance. His bright eyes
are intent; his eager body quivers. Suddenly he begins to run
from the group, flying over the green grass, his legs carrying
him faster and faster.

You have been spotted, and when you and your special friend
finally meet, you cling together in joyous reunion, never to
be parted again. The happy kisses rain upon your face; your
hands again caress the beloved head, and you look once more
into the trusting eyes of your pet, so long gone from your life
but never absent from your heart.

Then you cross Rainbow Bridge together. . . .

Truth be told, I couldn't help but find "The Rainbow Bridge" a little on the sugary side. But I knew that the poem was popular, which was why I included a mention of it in my piece all the same.

I received far and away more mail for "Will My Pet Go to Heaven?" than I had for any other piece of writing I'd done for *Guideposts*. People—in astonishing numbers—wrote in to thank me for stating what they'd long known but had despaired of ever hearing from someone else: yes, animals go to heaven; end of story.

One of the things I found most surprising in those letters was how often people told me that though they personally believed animals had souls, they felt they shouldn't be too vocal about this fact. Many people said they kept their feelings secret for fear of being made fun of. With some surprise, I realized that countless earnest, unapologetic, Bible-reading Christians out there—people who would happily tell a perfect stranger about their faith without a care as to whether that person judged them for it or not—felt strangely embarrassed about confessing their belief that not just people, but animals too, enjoyed a future life beyond the body.

Several veterinarians wrote to say that they had photocopied my article and placed stacks of it in their waiting rooms. "I've been practicing veterinary medicine for twenty years," one of those vets told me. "I know that what you wrote in your article is true. But many of my clients who've lost their animal companions hear different from their clergy. They go to them hoping to be reassured that their pet is safe in heaven, and that they'll see them again someday. But the pastors often tell them just the opposite. 'Animals don't have souls. Your pet is gone forever and you're just going to have to learn to come to terms with that.' It crushes the owners. Your article shows that there's strong scriptural evidence that animals survive death, and though I've long been convinced of that myself, it's a message I've never seen spelled out before."

But the most common sort of letter came from *Guideposts* readers who, because they weren't computer-savvy, had not seen "The Rainbow Bridge." Many of these people told me they'd heard tell of this wonderful piece of writing, but had never seen it. Could I send them a copy?

I printed out a dozen copies of "The Rainbow Bridge" and sent them off to everyone who asked. Then a dozen more. I was happy to oblige these people, but I couldn't help feeling puzzled each time I sealed up yet another envelope. Why were people so nuts about this piece of writing? The title alone seemed enough to instantly ignite their interest.

One day, folding up yet another copy of "The Rainbow Bridge" for yet another *Guideposts* reader who couldn't wait to get her hands on it, I stopped and read the whole thing through one more time. I still found it a little cloying, but I suddenly saw something in it—something that had been right there in front of me but that I'd somehow missed each time I'd read it before. "The Rainbow Bridge" might have been corny, but, language aside, it was making an entirely valid and vital spiritual point. The world is a profoundly happy-sad place. It is sad because we are currently cut off from a larger, more spiritual world to which we used to be intimately connected. And it is happy because the division that separates us from that larger existence, though terrible and huge, is crossable. There is a bridge between the worlds, one that is open to both humans *and* animals, and on it all people and animals will one day be reunited.

The vision of this heavenly reunion lay at the heart of all the spiritual traditions I'd been learning about over the years that took the animal soul seriously. From Khmwum, the elephant god of the Pygmies of Gabon who took the form of a rainbow, to the cosmic trees and mountains navigated by the shamans of Siberia, to the rainbow that Genesis tells us God set in the sky after the great flood, the same essential ideas and images that were in "The Rainbow Bridge" had been popping up everywhere since time immemorial. Whether it appealed to my literary tastes or not, "The Rainbow Bridge" was telling people what they knew in their hearts already, and had only been waiting for someone else to tell them as well: humans and animals are both soul beings, living and struggling in a world where they are momentarily—but only momentarily—separated from a heaven where they both equally belong.

Meanwhile, until the day when that separation is healed, animals and humans need each other. They need each other for companionship, but also because each has something to contribute about the knowledge of the world above this world that the other lacks. Animals understand heaven better than we do to an extent because they are, in their grace, their natural dignity, and their intuitive purity, quite simply closer to it than we are. And we in turn understand it better because we are microcosms of the Great Chain of Being itself, possessed of minds uniquely capable of fathoming and addressing both our own situation and that of animals within the cosmos. That's one reason why, when humans and animals do truly meet down here on earth, the combination of their different sensibilities, their different but equally real styles of intelligence, can have such a strange, haunting, and curiously powerful quality. As people like Jack and Patti Becklund know so well, whenever humans forge a truly spiritual connection with animals, the space separating earth from heaven becomes just a little smaller. And that fact alone is enough to make even the saddest animal story a happy one.

The Evidence Grows

A Dream Unlike Other Dreams

Most of the arguments of philosophy in favor of the immortality of man apply equally to the permanency of the immortal principle in living beings. May I not add that a future life in which man should be deprived of that great source of enjoyment, and intellectual and moral improvement, which result from the contemplation of the harmonies of an organic world, would involve a lamentable loss; and may we not look to a spiritual concert of the combined worlds and all their inhabitants in the presence of their Creator, as the highest conception of paradise?

—*Jean Louis Agassiz (1807–1873)*

Wherever you are going, they are going too.

—*James Herriot (1916–1995)*

Guideposts articles—even the pieces like "Will My Pet Go to Heaven?" that are structured like essays—usually include a story by the author to make them more homey and personal. To personalize the piece, I started off by talking about Angus, the rabbit responsible for everything I'd discovered about the animal soul so far. I described how I came to have him, how fond I got of him, and how sad I was on the day Sarah and I came home to find him dead in his cage. (Lamentably, *Guideposts* decency strictures forced me to leave Sarah, unmarried live-in girlfriend that she was, out of the story.)

It might have been all those personal details about Angus I'd included that made so many readers want to write me with stories of their own. I received dozens, most from readers who wanted to tell me how sad they had been when they'd lost their own pets.

A surprising number of those letters didn't just end with the death of the pets in question, however. They went on to describe experiences these people had had in the wake of those deaths—experiences that convinced many of them that their animals were not gone completely after all. A typical one ran:

> I was crushed when my fifteen-year-old white Persian Mindy died in my arms two years ago. My kids are grown, my husband died some years back, and Mindy was all I had in the world. I honestly didn't know if I could continue without her.
>
> One night a week or so after Mindy left me, I had an almost unbelievably vivid dream. In it, Mindy was curled in my arms just as she always used to be in life. Her body was young and healthy again, her coat bright and shiny, her big yellow eyes clear and sharp as diamonds. She looked up at me, and in those diamond eyes of hers I saw something—something I'll never forget. Mindy was communicating with me. I'd often felt, when she was alive, that

Mindy knew what I was thinking, and I was pretty good at reading her thoughts too. Well, there was no doubt in my mind what Mindy was telling me with that look. *I'm still here*—that's what she was saying. *Even though you can't see me or touch me anymore, my spirit is with you—and always will be.*

The dream was so vivid that it jolted me awake. My eyes popped open, and I found myself lying in bed. The whole room was filled with something. I don't know what you'd call it—an atmosphere, maybe. But I knew what it was. It was Mindy's spirit. It was there with me in the room. I just lay there quietly, thanking God for what he'd shown me. Finally I fell asleep. The next morning I knew the minute I opened my eyes that something was different. The feeling in the room was gone, but my view of the world had changed—for good.

Most people think of "visions" as dramatic, otherworldly events that happen only to highly exceptional people in highly exceptional circumstances. But visions aren't *always* huge and imposing and exalted, nor do they happen just to hermits, saints, people lost at sea, and mentally unstable romantic poets. They also happen to ordinary people in the most ordinary situations and places.

That, at least, was what a lot of the mail I got from readers suggested.

"The ad read 'German Shepherd/Dachshund mix puppy—free to good home,'" wrote a *Guideposts* reader and occasional contributor named Marni Rader.

Well, that I had to see. The puppy turned out to look like a dachshund but with a bigger body and longer legs. Rawley grew to thirty pounds and was obsessed with anything edible (which to him included soap stolen from the bathtub and gum stolen out of my purse). I once bought him an automatic feeder—one that would open at a certain time if I wasn't home. But my neighbor noticed through my kitchen window that he would just sit and stare at it all day while I was at work, waiting for it to open.

His other great love was a bowling ball I bought for him after he punctured every plastic ball I bought. I only let him play with it outside to keep him from smashing it into all the furniture in the house. His inability to destroy it frustrated him and he gouged deep grooves in it with his teeth. I'd let him play with it for a couple of hours until he rubbed the skin off his nose from pushing it around. Amazingly he could lift it by putting his teeth in the finger holes.

I took Rawley with me when I taught English in Japan for two years. My vet bent the rules and sent a two-year supply of phenobarbital with me, making me promise I would never take it. It was for controlling Rawley's occasional seizures after being diagnosed with epilepsy.

One night, years later and back in the states, Rawley's seizuring woke me up. He had fallen asleep with his head on my shoulder. I tried to give him his pills but he wouldn't swallow them. I had just moved to a new part of town in Orange County, California, and hadn't found a new vet yet. I grabbed the Yellow Pages and frantically searched for the nearest animal hospital. I woke up my husband and we raced down the freeway. On the way there, lying in my arms, Rawley died.

I called in sick to work the next day. Every day coming home to an empty house drove me straight into the bedroom to weep. I agonized over not being able to get Rawley to the hospital in time and couldn't stop wondering about where he was now—and if he was okay.

One night after I'd fallen asleep in tears as usual, missing that warm furry body next to me, Rawley came to me. Running in his funny lopsided way, ears flapping. It was a dream, and yet it was more than a dream. It was *him*—really and truly. I hugged and kissed Rawley, and watched him dashing through the grass in the sunshine. I felt his joy. He was absolutely okay and he had come to reassure me of that. I woke up knowing without a doubt that he was happy, that he loved me, and that I would see him again someday. I only lasted two months before getting my next dog, a miniature pinscher named Tinker. Tinker will be ten years old this year, and while she is healthy and has lots of life left, I'm not as worried about her passing. Because I know that when she does, she will have a friend to greet her.

Out of the Closet

Dream visions of recently deceased pets weren't, by this point, an entirely new phenomenon to me. Sharon at the office had told me of several she'd had when dogs of hers died, and I'd also read about them in Scott Smith's *The Soul of Your Pet*, one of those books on the animal soul that I'd picked up in the course

of my recent researches. Smith had put a query in several magazines asking for stories from people who had had experiences
that led them to believe animals survived death. The surprise he
experienced at the mail he got was similar to what I'd felt after
my *Guideposts* piece had come out.

"I was," Smith wrote, "stunned by the response. Rather than
'ghost stories' you could dismiss as the result of overworked
imaginations, the reports which came in were amazing in their
variety, complexity and credibility. Experiences were sometimes
lengthy and multi-sensory, occurring to perfectly normal people
who usually did not have supernatural experiences of any kind."

These kinds of events, Smith suggested, were actually quite
common, but one didn't hear about them for the simple reason
that people were shy about discussing them. "As I talked and
wrote about the accumulating evidence for animal immortality,"
Smith wrote, "more and more people would approach me with
new stories. It became clear that there is a tremendous reservoir
of experiences of this sort, that people are just now coming out
of the closet about these things, as happened two decades ago
with near-death experiences. The door has now been cracked
open and there is obviously much left to learn."

Most of the visions described in Smith's book matched the
kind I was hearing about from *Guideposts* readers. Shortly after
losing a much-loved pet, the individual involved experiences a
singularly vivid dream, one in which they see the animal they
have lost, happy and healthy in some bright, pleasant environment like a field thick with grass and flowers. People typically
awake from these dreams suffused with a feeling of well-being.
They know—with a certainty that no one can talk them out

of—that their pet is okay. Very often they also have the equally firm conviction that they will see their pet again someday.

Though they didn't identify it by name, I realized that many of the pet visions I encountered—both in books and in the letters I received—occurred while the people concerned were in the hypnagogic state, that strange zone between waking and sleep in which we're not quite conscious but not quite unconscious, either, the place where what are sometimes called waking dreams take place. The word *hypnagogia* comes from combining the Greek words for "sleep" (*hypnos*) and "conductor" (*agogeus*). This root suggests that the hypnagogic state has important things to teach us, that it can lead us, as it were, to important new places, and this has, in fact, been the general feeling about hypnagogia since ancient times. The third-century Greek philosopher Iamblichus called the visions that occur in this state "god-sent," and even Aristotle remarked upon them, writing in *De Somniis* that "in the moment of awakening" a man may "surprise the images which present themselves to him in sleep."

Most of us experience the hypnagogic state at least twice a day—in the morning when we exit the world of sleep and in the evening when we enter it again. But, as the psychologist Wilson Van Dusen points out in his book *The Presence of Other Worlds*, few people "ever pause at this level to explore the spontaneous wellsprings of mind bubbling forth. This state is a delicate balance of self-awareness and the presence of inner processes. . . . The same symbolism that appears in dreams appears in the hypnagogic state. But one can't normally talk to or deal with dreams. There is enough self-awareness in the hypnagogic state to remember, record, and even talk to inner processes."

These "inner processes" may involve more than a simple plunge into the amorphous contents of the subconscious mind. Theorists who hold to the idea that consciousness itself evolves have suggested that when we pass through the hypnagogic zone, we are actually accessing an earlier state of consciousness: one that our Paleolithic ancestors (who, in line with the evolution-of-consciousness theory, genuinely experienced a different world than we do) may have enjoyed much more extended access to. This earlier state of consciousness in which the individual experienced him- or herself as more immersed in the world, less cut off from its energies and spiritual personages, may have at least partially inspired the dreamlike quality of so many of the animal images that float across the roofs and walls of the Paleolithic caves. On the edge of sleep, as the normally rock-solid borders between the inner "me" and the world "out there" grow weaker, we recover, for a moment, this old style of consciousness. No longer locked within that highly efficient, highly defined, yet also unspeakably cramped and limited sense of self that all of us in the modern world have been taught to inhabit, we break free for a moment, our inner "me" coming back to its old strength and integrity like a flopping sea creature that someone has picked from the floor of a boat and tossed back into the water.

It's in this state that many a bereaved pet owner has found him or herself "talking" to a departed pet, and "listening" to them, too—even though no actual words are passed. A bereaved dog owner might see her formerly ill and aged dog not only in a pleasant environment, but young and vigorous again as well. These visions typically convey two things to the grieving owner: first, the pets involved are still "there"—that is, they still exist, even if not down on the material plane; and, second, they are just fine. In fact, *better* than fine.

The Sleeping Dachshund

Hypnagogic states, real as they are to the people who experience them, are easy for naysayers to deal with. How surprising, after all, is it for a grieving pet owner to have a dream about his or her deceased companion? Less easy to dismiss are the visions that people have when they're fully awake. I classified these kinds "sleeping dachshund" stories, after one in which a woman who, heartbroken after the loss of her aged dachshund, one day looked over at the dog's bed (which she'd been too sad to remove) and saw it happily curled up there.

These kinds of experiences, while not as common as dream visions, are nonetheless much more common than one might suspect. So, too, are experiences in which less well defined visual phenomena—things like smoke, mist, or strange lights—appear just before, after, or during an animal's death. In *The Soul of Your Pet*, Smith tells the story of a veterinary technician named Scott McKinney. In 1983, McKinney was called on to help with the euthanasia of a severely ill Doberman pinscher. "He was a beautiful dog," McKinney relates, "and I admit I cried, not for having to euthanize him, but for his release from pain."

The dog was put down, and McKinney prepared to bag the body and put it in the holding freezer. Looking at the dead animal, McKinney "beheld the most beautiful sight: out of his body came a luminous haze. It clung to the body ever so slightly, then, in one snap, became a cloud over his old body. He bounced around the body for a minute and then slowly joined two more 'clouds' that appeared, before they all disappeared."

Clouds, smoke, and mysterious lights show up frequently, of course, in the literature on human ghosts and apparitions. Such phenomena are often connected to the etheric body—the lowest and most physical of several "spiritual" bodies believed to exist by various occult and esoteric traditions. If—as we've been doing throughout this book—we picture the physical and spiritual dimensions as a hierarchy, the etheric is the spiritual zone that's right above the physical. The two are so close together, and influence each other so directly, it's theorized, that people who are sensitive to such things can see glints and flashes of the etheric playing at the edges of objects in the physical world all the time.

One particularly interesting story relating to the etheric occurs in the famous psychic Eileen Garrett's 1949 book *Adventures in the Supernormal*. After the suicide of her parents, Garrett was entrusted to an aunt, who punished the young girl after she reported seeing ghosts. Garrett was so angry at the punishment that she decided to take revenge on her aunt by killing her favorite ducklings. Garrett writes:

> Bending over the edge of the pond, I caught each small duckling as it came floating by and held each one under water, one after another, till I had drowned the entire brood. I laid them in a row on the grass beside me, and as I contemplated them I became filled with a terrible dread of the wrath to come. I felt now that God himself might come

to punish me for this, and I remained rooted to the spot, frozen with fear, awaiting the force of his anger. The very intensity of my fear created a state of suspended quietness in which I seemed scarcely to breathe, yet I was alert and waiting, anticipating the final overwhelming disaster.

In this condition I gazed at the little bodies lying on the grass, half hoping that somehow they might still be alive. The little dead bodies were quiet, but a strange movement was occurring all about them. A gray smoke-like substance rose up from each small form. This nebulous, fluid stuff wove and curled as it rose in winding spiral curves, and I saw it take new shape as it moved out and away from the quiet forms. As I watched the spectacle, fear gave way to amazement. I became almost joyful, for I thought the ducklings were coming alive again, and I waited in tense expectancy.

The ducklings did not come back to life. Thanks perhaps to that "state of suspended quietness" in which she found herself, however, Garrett was, it seems, able to catch a glimpse of that moment of overlap that occurs when a living body—whether animal or human—turns into a dead one, and the life—the *nephesh*—that animated it moves on.

Another story of a vision occurring while the person concerned was fully awake—one mercifully less morbid than Garrett's—came to me in the mail at *Guideposts* from an Alabama woman named Patricia.

Tears filled my eyes as I walked away from Magic, the horse I had dreamed of owning ever since I'd first seen

Black Beauty as a kid. When I bought Magic she was two years old and she'd already been abused. My life had been pretty much the same. In Magic I found a true soul mate.

But I wasn't a kid anymore. I was now divorced, and as a single parent I needed to focus on the job of raising my two children. Money was tight. Everything had to be budgeted very carefully. I was forced to sell Magic, along with my son's sweet pony, Judge. The two horses were inseparable. Now they would be apart.

How I missed all the good times Magic and I had—especially the feeling of the wind against us as I rode her through the fields. Years went by, but I never forgot my incredible friend. One day I had a chance to visit her. As I walked up to the fence, I whistled for her, and called out her name. She came right away. As she got closer, I noticed she didn't have the same bounce in her step. My heart sank. My sweet horse, once muscular and strong, was wasting away.

I tried to buy Magic back, but the owner said he didn't want to sell her. I even fed her under cover of darkness. My children grew up, and when they moved out to start lives of their own, the sadness in my heart for Magic was almost more than I could bear.

Then one day I learned that the person who owned Magic was having financial problems and would be willing to sell her. It was almost too good to be true. The beautiful black mare I had loved and missed for so many years would be mine again. When I came to pick her up, the sadness both she and I had held in our hearts seemed to vanish in a moment. Magic didn't even wait for me to load her onto the horse trailer. She trotted ahead and jumped on herself. After fourteen long years my beloved horse and I were together again.

It was just like old times. We played tag in the pasture, shared ice cream cones and sweet tea. I felt like a kid again—and clearly so did Magic.

Magic loved challenges, so one day I decided to teach her some tricks: shake hands, pray, give a kiss, shake her head No . . . stuff like that. She picked up on the tricks so fast—it was like she could read my mind. Not too long after I'd taught Magic her tricks, God sent a woman into my life who was the director of a single mother's ministry. I began to take Magic to local festivals to show off her stuff. The money we made, we gave to the single mom's ministry. God not only gave me back my horse, he gave me the tools to help another group of people dear to my heart: single moms.

At 27, Magic became ill and the vet said the only kind thing to do would be to put her to sleep. I sat with her as the vet administered the shot, stroking her neck, tears streaming down my cheeks. As Magic passed from this world, I had what I can only describe as a vision. It was completely real—*more* than real. Magic was standing in a field as another horse came out to greet her. In a moment I recognized the horse as Judge—the little pony Magic had been so close to years before. The two horses nuzzled, then both reared up and took off together, manes flying.

Magic had the same markings as the horse in *Black Beauty*: a white star on her forehead, and a white left hind pastern. I didn't realize it till, after Magic's passing, I bought and re-watched the DVD. She truly was the horse God had meant for me to have. In this life, we can never be totally free from worry for the ones we love. But that's not true in the life to come. We'll be reunited there with the people we love, and the animals too. I'm comforted to know that when my time comes, I'll have a young, strong, beautiful horse to carry me across that great divide. Magic and I will never be separated again.

Morphic Fields

The etheric dimension and the forces at work there are similar—or perhaps identical—to what the British biologist Rupert Sheldrake calls "morphic fields": invisible, all-pervasive nets of nonmaterial intelligence that direct the growth and activity of all organic life. These fields, Sheldrake believes, are responsible for everything smart in nature, from the size and shape of a hummingbird's wing to a young orangutan's innate knowledge that snakes are to be avoided.

Morphic fields also sound a lot, to some ears—especially those of Sheldrake's many and highly vocal critics in the scientific community—like the ancient forces of soul and spirit, revived and brought back into the realm of modern science. Sheldrake doesn't disagree. The ancients, he wrote in his controversial 1989 book *The Presence of the Past*, were correct when they suggested that "the world and all living beings within it are animate, in other words that they are organized by non-material souls or psyches or animas." Sheldrake believes that all of nature is deeply teleonomic—a fancy way of saying that it is not blind or dumb, but knows very well what it is doing at all times. "Soul," for him, is a kind of vast, invisible memory bank that saves information from the past and uses it to mold the bodies and guide the actions of all living organisms—from bacteria all the way up to human beings.

Where did this intelligence come from? Sheldrake doesn't claim to know. But he does suggest (and this has gotten him into trouble not only with mainstream scientists but with proponents of traditional religion as well) that not only is everything in the cosmos changing and evolving all the time, but so, too, are the actual rules by which these changes operate. Far from being static and unchangeable, the laws that govern nature are essentially as open to change as the productions of nature themselves. "Why," asks Sheldrake, "should matter, energy, nature, life, or process be creative? This is inevitably mysterious. Not much more can be said than that it is their nature to be so."

Sheldrake's willingness to actually type the word *soul* without immediately dismissing the possibility that it could refer to something real separates him from a fair number of his fellow scientists. But because Sheldrake *is* a scientist, his work has stopped short of attempting to answer the most central and mysterious question raised by all paranormal phenomena: *What happens, at the death of an animal or a human, to the individual personality?*

Lingering Spirits

Ghostly apparitions—whether of animals or people—don't necessarily answer this question either, for the simple reason

that ghosts themselves are often not all that . . . *personal.* Just
as continents, in their millennia-long drift across the face of the
planet, can leave islands behind them—broken-off pieces of
earth that still reflect the geological peculiarities of the larger
body that has moved on—so it might be that the soul, in moving from life to death, can leave fragments of itself in its wake
as well: impersonal, mechanical entities that—like the shades
of early Greek and Hebrew religion—are a far cry from the
fully realized personality that had once lived on earth. This is
why parapsychological researchers and various other students
of the supernatural often refer to ghosts as "husks"—discarded,
semi-animate, semiconscious containers of the more complex
spiritual essence that has now departed. This view does a good
job of explaining why, in the stories told of them, ghosts so often
seem to be such dullards. Rather than doing or saying anything
interesting, these apparitions simply stop and stare dumbly at
the observer for a moment before going back to whatever activity they were engaged in before they were spotted. Ghosts—or
at least these sorts of ghosts—are more like etheric footprints
left behind by the full personality that has died and departed, and
it's possible that some animal apparitions, like those persistent
but behaviorally hidebound hounds and horses that are often reported to haunt the grounds of crumbling Southern plantations
and suchlike places, fit this bill as well.

Not all human ghosts, however, behave the same way. Though
many human ghosts move in an empty, automatic manner that
suggests they are indeed mere shells or husks of the full personality that used to inhabit them, others appear to have a little
more substance to them.

The same goes for animal ghosts. Take the ghostly deer that
Bill D. Schul describes in *Animal Immortality,* a book that came
out in 1990, just after my inconclusive visit to the City Lights
bookstore. Schul was on a group meditation retreat in Colorado
at the time of his encounter, in a remote spot boasting a number
of especially large blue spruces. One evening during the retreat,
Schul slipped away from his companions to go sit beneath one
of these trees. "It was a hauntingly beautiful night," he writes,
"and I decided to meditate on my special piece of earth.

"I had not meditated for long when something made me open
my eyes. Not twenty-five feet from me, walking slowly along the
road, was a deer." Earlier in the day Schul had encountered a
large buck nearby, and at first he thought it was that same animal. "But as the deer drew closer I realized it was much smaller
than the buck I had seen earlier. It seemed to be aware of my
presence, for it paused on the path and seemed to be looking in
my direction. When it stopped, I was startled to find that not
only was I looking at the deer but I was also looking through it.
The deer appeared real enough except for the transparent quality of the body, for I could clearly see the shadowy bushes on the
edge of the road directly through him.

"I mentally asked him to come closer, but his only response
was a momentary pause to look back in my direction as he continued unhurriedly up the path in the moonlight. A hundred or
so feet up the road he turned into the woods and disappeared."

The event lingered in Schul's mind. Though it only gave him a
glance before walking on, the way a typical "husk" variety ghost
might, Schul sensed a connection with the ghost animal that gave
the whole event a strangely personal and intimate flavor. The

following year, Schul described his encounter to a modern-day shamanic practitioner who was visiting the retreat spot as well. This individual told Schul that "when animals die, their essence may be more strongly attached to physical existence than that of most humans. It may take them some time to experience reality beyond the earth plane. They linger here in their astral state until a sufficient part of their being is ready to move on. The earth plane is inhabited by many phantom animals but most people are not aware of them, although their own kind may be."

Etheric bodies, astral states, and other such concepts are generally relegated to the category of occultism these days, and as such are ignored both by scientists and mainstream believers in traditional faiths as well. This is unfortunate, because if the universe really does possess a spiritual aspect, there is no reason to imagine that it is in any way hazy, amorphous, or less real than the physical.

The Imaginal Dimension

Help in learning how to appreciate the detailed, specific, and in every way non-vague world of the more-than-physical dimensions is available not just from modern occult/esoteric thought, but from the world's spiritual traditions as well. A number of Islamic mystics have described a spiritual zone above and beyond the earthly landscape where the rules of perception are different from those that govern the mundane world. This zone goes by many names, but one of the most suggestive, employed by the French scholar of Islamic and pre-Islamic Iranian spiritual traditions Henry Corbin, is the *imaginal.*

In using this name, Corbin did not mean to suggest that the events that take place within the imaginal dimension are imaginary, but only that they require imagination in order to be perceived. All perception—even the ordinary, everyday variety—requires our mental participation. The daily world we all take for granted, Corbin points out, is much more of a collaborative affair than most of us normally assume it is. The earthly sights, sounds, smells, textures, and tastes that flood in through our senses every day do not arrive ready-made, but require considerable—if largely unconscious—mental assembly before we can consciously experience them in a unified and coherent way. The same, says Corbin, is true of the events that happen on the imaginal plane; they just require a little *more* assembly. (That's why Corbin terms the faculty we use to apprehend this dimension the "active imagination," and that's also why the things people see in this dimension can be real even though they're in part created by the personal imagination of the observer.)

Of the many interesting things that could be said about the imaginal world, perhaps the most important for our purposes is that everything one encounters there (from rocks and trees to buildings and even entire cities) has a distinctly *personal* quality to it. As Corbin says, the pronoun best used when describing the specifics of this dimension is not "what" but "who." (The conscious trees and teapots found in fairy tales are nods to this dimension, as are the talking furniture in *Pee-wee's Playhouse* and the animated objects that jump and dance around in the *Shrek* films.)

The imaginal dimension, Corbin wrote (understating the matter considerably), is "a universe for which it is difficult in our language to find a satisfactory term." It is "an 'external world,' and yet it is not the physical world. It is a world that teaches us that it is possible to emerge from measurable space without emerging from extent, and that we must abandon homogeneous chronological time in order to enter that qualitative time which is the history of the soul."

To call the imaginal zone the place where heaven and earth overlap just a little would be a tad simplistic—but it would also be true. It would also be more in line with traditional Christianity and Judaism than we might at first suspect. A glance at both the Hebrew Bible and the New Testament with Corbin's ideas in mind reveals countless passages that the theory of the imaginal dimension can help to clarify. Who or what were the three strangers who visited Abraham under the oaks of Mamre in Genesis? In what state of mind or perception did Moses witness the burning bush on the side of Mount Horeb? And what of the countless spiritual beings and presences described in the letters of Paul? Were these beings and events imaginary? Were they real? Perhaps, Corbin would suggest, they were both.

The Role of Psychical Research

Another controversial but extremely fruitful perspective on the animal soul is provided by that group of investigators into the paranormal that fall under the general heading of psychical researchers. Psychical research, and the movement of spiritualism that is closely related to it, has a spotty image these days, and tends to conjure up scenes of bored, gullible nineteenth-century society men and women gazing idly into crystals or consulting

Ouija boards. But in its heyday in the late nineteenth and early twentieth centuries, psychical research boasted a long list of students—including Sherlock Holmes's creator Arthur Conan Doyle and the psychologist William James—who were neither dumb nor bored nor especially gullible.

Drawing their conclusions from what they learned through trance mediums—the ancestors of today's new-age channelers—these researchers put together a picture of the spiritual world that in broad outline is very similar to the one we have been sketching in this book. Like Plato, the early Church Fathers, and most of the world's shamans, the spiritualists envisioned the world as a multilevel affair, with matter lying at the very bottom. Stretching "above" the physical world (though we have to take the word metaphorically, as these worlds were not thought to literally exist in the sky but rather on different levels of reality) was, the spiritualists maintained, a series of more-refined worlds of ever-increasing subtlety and beauty.

The most important of these ascending levels for our purposes is the one that lies immediately above the physical world—an exceedingly pleasant realm of green fields and sunshine into which most people—excepting rare individuals with exceptionally cruel and evil natures—pass upon dying. This realm goes by many names in spiritualist literature, from the misleading "Land of Illusion" (for what happens there is not so much illusory as it is co-created by our imaginations) to the classical "Elysium" to my personal favorite, "Summerland."

In essence, this first stop on the spiritualist map of the soul's ascent is identical to the earth-above-the-earth envisioned by the shaman. It is a place very much like earth, and newly dead people are said to often mistake it at first for earth itself. (My favorite anecdote from spiritualist literature illustrating this tenet concerns a deceased World War I soldier who remarked to one of his comrades that there was "something funny" about the cigarettes they were smoking. Having been killed in battle, the two were enjoying a post-combat smoke together without yet realizing that they had entered the world of spirit—where smoking continues to be permitted, at least on its lower levels.)

Easy as it is for newcomers to mistake it as such, Summerland is very definitely *not* the physical earth, but rather an improved "double" of it, in which the particular beings and objects that exist down here are reborn in spiritualized form. As recorded in a long-forgotten classic of spiritualist literature called *The Road to Immortality*, the deceased paranormal investigator F. W. H. Myers narrates to the medium Geraldine Cummins his experiences of this world in extraordinary detail. He describes the souls who dwell there as living "within the loom of earth still, in the sense that they dwell in the soul's dream of earth."

These souls are not human alone, but include, says the deceased Myers, those of animals as well. "For many departed souls," he reported through Cummins, "there is this dream-world here, this ether-image of the earth. It is a place built up out of the earthly memories of men, and possesses many of the geographical features of the earth. Many simple souls dwell contentedly in surroundings that appear to them as solid and substantial as the material shapes on earth. In this habitat, old dog friends or cats who were comrades in other days may gravitate again to their masters or mistresses by virtue of their affection for them, that is, if the masters or mistresses are living in this Shadow Land.

For we call it a 'Shadow Land,' though it is really far more beautiful than the earth. It is, in truth, the next state, and the journeying soul must pass through it, even though he may not tarry long within its borders."

Myers did not state that animals and humans dwelt forever in this enchanted place. It is, for him, a passage-point to realms above: realms that Myers found ever more difficult to describe in earthly terms, but that fit well with the ancient idea of a ladder of worlds, each more subtle and all-inclusive than the last.

The spiritualist narratives of the life beyond are not for everybody. But even for those of us who see in them no more than a deluded if poetic fancy, their similarity to the descriptions of the earth-above-the-earth provided by so many primordial peoples, along with so many historical philosophers, saints, and mystics, is haunting and impressive all the same. Reading "The Rainbow Bridge," hearing the descriptions of bereaved pet owners who have been comforted by astonishingly vivid dream visions of their pets alive and well in a green heaven of rolling fields and sunshine, one can't help but be impressed by the parallels between these stories and the spiritualist literature. The work of Myers and other spiritualist authors—both living and deceased—shows once again that there is a powerful universality to our beliefs about the beyond, and the place that animals might hold there.

Help from Beyond

Does one, a reader might ask at this point, really need to get into such daunting areas of philosophical speculation, not to mention seemingly bizarre beliefs like those of the spiritualists, in order to explain the kinds of experiences I heard about from *Guideposts* readers and discovered in books like Bill Schul's and Scott Smith's? Might one not be better off chalking all these experiences up to plain, simple, earthly grief combined with regular, run-of-the-mill, earthly imagination? In the end, how a person answers this question might depend more on his or her native temperament than on anything else. You're either the type of person who's ready to believe in such things . . . or you're not.

Some encounters with ghost pets, however, have such an unarguable urgency and intensity to them that they can make questions of their reality seem academic at best. Take, for example, the stories of animals that haven't simply comforted the humans to whom they appear, but actually helped them.

In his book, Schul includes several stories about this kind of animal ghost; the following, reported by Lowanda Cady of Wichita, Kansas, is typical. Lowanda lived in an apartment complex in an area that was being repeatedly targeted by a burglar who made a habit of stealing food from refrigerators. Late one night she was awakened by her dog Jock's agitated barking downstairs. She heard hurried footsteps, then the sound of a door opening. "Mrs. Cady," writes Schul, "investigated and discovered that an intruder had been helping himself to the contents of her refrigerator. She started to look for Jock and stopped, having temporarily forgotten in the excitement that her pet had died three months before."

Stories of ghost animals who return to help a grieving owner, while not as plentiful as stories of vivid dreams in which a pet returns to comfort and reassure its master, aren't uncommon

ravens, whales, dolphins, and even social insects like ants and bees certainly qualify as language by most definitions of the word. But the degree to which some psychic-intuitive animal communicators take for granted the ability of animals to speak betrays a certain lack of respect for the essential mystery and otherness of even the most thoroughly domesticated animals. The testimonies of these contemporary animal communicators seem—to me at least—to suggest that if animals could speak they would order and express their thoughts just as we humans do. And that assumption really cheapens more than deepens our understanding of the true shape and nature of the animal soul.

All the same, some people who claim to have the gift of animal communication do exhibit a certain undeniable believability. J. Allen Boone's *Kinship with All Life,* beloved by countless readers since its publication in 1954, detailed Boone's wordless communications with creatures ranging from a famous German shepherd named Strongheart to a housefly named Freddie.

People of ancient times, writes Boone, expressing an idea that should certainly sound familiar by this point,

> appear to have been great virtuosos in the art of living, particularly skilled in the delicate science of being in right relations with everything, including animals. . . . They refused to make any separate barriers between mineral and vegetable, between vegetable and man, or between man and the great Primal Cause which animates and governs all things. Every living thing was seen as a partner in a universal enterprise. . . . Those were the days when "the whole earth was of one language and speech . . . and all was one grand

concord." Humans, animals, snakes, birds, insects—all shared a common language. . . . There is evidence that at one time on earth every living thing was able to be in rational correspondence with everything else. Humans and animals moved in full accord not only with one another but with the cosmic Plan as well.

One of Boone's practices during his stint as the German shepherd Strongheart's caretaker was a highly unusual one: he read to the dog for an hour each day, just as my stepbrother Nicky's teacher Rinpoche had with Jack Benny. "Every morning," Boone writes, "Strongheart and I would sit facing each other . . . and I would share the contents of books, magazines, and newspapers with him, taking care that he got the best in subject matter as well as in literary expression." By reading to the dog, Boone felt, he was "mentally lifting him out of all kinds of limiting dog classifications and balancing life with him as an intelligent fellow being."

Boone ultimately decided to reverse the customary dog-man relationship with Strongheart and make himself the dog's pupil. What Boone learned from this experiment sounds very much like a synthesis of Paleolithic and Platonic attitudes toward what animals are, and one that any full and complete philosophy of the animal soul would do well to keep in mind:

"When we first began living together," Boone writes, "my attitude toward Strongheart had been the conventional one. I assigned myself a place high on the scale of values because I was a 'human,' and gave him a place far below because he happened to be 'a dog.' " But "when I began my 'dog-trains-man' experiment with Strongheart, I was compelled to learn that if I wanted to achieve complete awareness of him, or of any other living thing, I would have to use something far more penetrating and perceptive with which to see than just a couple of eyeballs in my skull . . . I had to discard my eyeballs . . . so to speak, and to begin using my thinking to see with."

Boone notes that the wisest figures throughout history have agreed that "our five organs of sense give us a kind of 'feel' of the universe and the various things that it contains, but they do not help us to experience things as they really are. Rather the sense organs distort the reality, as if we were trying to view and understand a beautiful landscape through a camera lens that is out of focus. . . . Penetrating deep into the mysteries of every kind of phenomena in their search for true answers," these explorers discovered "that behind every object that the senses can identify, whether the object be human, animal, tree, mountain, plant or anything else . . . is the mental and spiritual fact functioning in all its completeness and perfection."

It was by using this primary style of perception that Boone was able, at last, to see Strongheart for what he really was: a fellow spiritual being clothed in the body of a dog. The more Boone practiced this way of looking, "the more I lifted my concept of Strongheart out of the physical and into the mental, and out of the mental into the spiritual."

One day, "just for fun," Boone decided to conduct an "interview" with Strongheart. "I went to work on him as a reporter," he writes, "talking across to him mentally in order not to disturb the sanctuary stillness in which we were both sitting, aiming all that I soundlessly said at the back of his head. I asked him questions having to do with his most intimate life, with me, with us, with human-animal relationships. There was no sequence in the questioning. I asked whatever came to mind. I did not wait for answers; I really did not expect any.

"Eventually I ran out of things to ask him. I relaxed into a pleasing feeling of suspended animation and a blank state of mind. Suddenly, and without the least sound from me to attract his attention, Strongheart swung his head around and began staring at me, and right through me, with those big eyes of his. It was unexpected—and startling."

Time seemed to stop as Strongheart kept his eyes focused on Boone. "Presently Strongheart turned his head back to its original position and calmly resumed looking off into space. And then—as easily and naturally as though such things were a regular part of everyday experience—I knew that Strongheart had been silently talking back to me. And I had actually been able to understand what he had said to me!"

Boone's conclusion? "I had spoken to Strongheart in the kind of speech which does not have to be uttered or written, and he had replied to me in the same language. . . . I had at last made contact with that seemingly lost universal silent language which, as those illumined ancients pointed out long ago, all life is innately equipped to speak with all life whenever minds and hearts are properly attuned."

Boone's kinship with Strongheart was so intense and personal that it continued, Boone reports, after Strongheart died. Man and dog remained intuitively bound after Strongheart left his physical body behind, and Boone even penned a book of letters to his deceased friend, each one addressed:

To
Strongheart
Eternal Playground
Out Yonder

"Let others believe you are dead if they desire," wrote Boone in the first of these letters to his old friend. "That is their privilege. But I want no part of it; for as far as I am concerned, you are just as vitally alive, and just as much the 'old pal' now as ever. It could not be otherwise. I know too much about the expanse of the real you."

A "Voice" from Beyond

Animal communicators like Boone are essentially modern shamans, and the messages that their communications deliver to us are, at their most convincing, identical to the messages delivered by the shamans and sages of ages past who went out into the wild to understand the thoughts of the animals they lived with. Boone was careful to emphasize that Strongheart's communications with him, both while he was on earth and after he left it behind, took place through a form of mystical-intuitive communion that essentially bypassed the need for actual spoken words. But many animal communicators today tell a different story about their own communications with animals, both dead and alive. It may be that the best, or at least most generous, way to understand telepathic/intuitive communication with animals that result in actual verbal messages is to remember that all of our experience is creative to a degree. Something, in this case, may really come from the animal—a wordless communication that the mind of the human communicator forms into words at an unconscious level, and then consciously receives as a fully formed, human-sounding sentence.

Such communications are most believable when they are direct and straightforward, and not covered over by human assumptions and attitudes. An animal psychic who advises a dog's owners that, for example, it is feeling anxiety over their recent divorce and wishes they could patch things up strikes me as far less easy to take seriously than one who delivers a message such as, "Bosko feels sad because you don't walk him as much as you used to." This isn't to say, of course, that animals aren't capable of complex feelings—only that it seems likely that the feelings they express psychically would not involve highly complex human concepts like romantic separation and reconciliation that simply don't exist among animals.

In *The Strange World of Animals and Pets*, Vincent and Margaret Gaddis give an unusual but oddly compelling example of this direct, "verbal" form of animal communication. Miss Anne Grazebrook, the authors tell us, while visiting her sister, encountered a dog named Bounce whom she felt pity for. Bounce was a mixed breed who lived on her sister's estate, and received little in the way of care and attention because he was a mere mutt. Grazebrook took pity on the animal, and the two struck up a friendship.

Sometime after leaving her sister's house, the Gaddises tell us, Grazebrook woke up in the early morning hours to the barking of a dog. It was, it seemed, right there in her bedroom.

"I sat up in bed," says Grazebrook, "and to my surprise I saw

Bounce. I put out my hand and felt him. He had his collar on and he was warm and solid to the touch. In utter astonishment I exclaimed, 'Bounce, how did you get here?' and a human voice replied, 'I was shot yesterday—I have come to say goodbye!' Then the dog was gone. How he came, how he went, whence came the voice, I could not say. I was left in a state of complete bewilderment."

A few weeks afterward, Grazebrook got a letter from her sister's governess telling her that Bounce had been shot and killed on the twenty-fourth of August. Bounce had appeared in Grazebrook's bedroom on the morning of the twenty-fifth.

"I can only add," Grazebrook said, "that at the time when I saw the dog, it did not occur to me even remotely that he was dead. His bark was loud enough to rouse me from a heavy sleep; he did not look distressed, merely excited as a dog might be at the sight of an old friend, and I can only repeat that when I patted him he was apparently alive and tangible beneath my hand."

Was Bounce talking? It seems unlikely. But in their telegram-like brevity and specificity, the words Grazebrook heard *do* sound like what her unconscious might have told her if it somehow telepathically picked up on the deceased dog's emotive intent.

Spiritual Science

Another unconventional approach to the idea of the animal soul from a scientific angle is provided by Wolfgang Schad, who has applied the researches of the Austrian philosopher and "spiritual scientist" Rudolf Steiner—founder of Anthroposophy and the Waldorf Schools—to an examination of the shape and character not just of the physical bodies of animals, but their soul bodies as well.

"If we observe the world of nature as it unfolds before our eyes, and at the same time study natural science with its abundance of information, we shall sooner or later," writes Schad, "come to the following realization: Today the immediate observation of nature and the study of natural science have generally become separate activities."

Schad believes this is an unfortunate development, and he has sought to study animals within the context of a worldview that, like that of Sheldrake, accepts the possibility of invisible forces that form and direct the lives of animals at all times. Schad's approach combines rigorous observation of living animals with what one might call a deliberately cultivated, meditative sympathy or openness to what one is looking at. This style of observation was pioneered in the eighteenth century by Johann Wolfgang von Goethe. Goethe believed that in observing nature we have to do so in a state of mind that allows the living forces within it (forces evocative of Plato's archetypes and Sheldrake's morphic fields) to genuinely penetrate our consciousness. As one commentator points out, the Goethe-Steiner approach to nature championed by Schad "requires the observer to be objective, as a scientist *must* be; but at the same time it calls upon him for an intuitive power of sympathetic identification. Every step forward in this kind of knowing strengthens the observer's rapport with the created world that confronts him."

What does such a collaborative observer discover at work in animals? The answers are often surprising, but just as often compelling. Consider Schad's highly original—and somehow strangely convincing—description of the soul life of a house mouse. "This animal," writes Schad, "is always more or less 'beside itself.' Whatever goes on around it is experienced intensively by the animal's soul, while its body remains unimportant, small, insignificant. How inadequately this animal seems to manage in its far too hastily formed body! An insatiable quest for food, constantly interrupted by terrified flight, fills its days. Frequent naps are required because of this constant nervous strain; yet these are of extremely short duration, and even in sleep shudders of excitement pass over the tiny, sleeping form. A rodent lives almost reluctantly, in a state of constant fear."

Compare this startling but oddly penetrating picture of the mouse to Schad's description of a cow. The soul activity of this animal, says Schad, is more interior, more anchored in the physical, than that of the mouse. "The cow," he writes, "gazes out upon the world as though through a veil of mist.... By its very nature the ungulate is a perennial optimist, even to its physiology. It could otherwise never be satisfied with its almost indigestible food. Such an animal is so self-sufficient that its emotional activity can be completely absorbed in the life of its own body. Much of the ungulate's soul life—despite its undoubted intensity and power—does not appear at the surface, because it is too much involved in the processes of digestion and growth to establish any close relationship with the outer world."

Schad's observations become stranger still when he turns his attentions to what happens when an animal dies. "What does the soul of an animal experience at death?" Schad asks. "We propose that these experiences are as diverse as the physical constitutions of the various animal species. An animal deeply tied to its own body dies with much greater difficulty than one closely connected with the outside world."

As an example, Schad cites that most familiar of predator-prey events: a cat catching a mouse.

"Death," says Schad, "comes to the mouse as a welcome release from a life filled with fear. An actual feeling of well-being accompanies its separation from the inadequate body to which it has felt chained. And the cat, when it plays for a while with the half-dead mouse, actually prolongs for the 'victim' this enjoyment of death! A more radical departure from all generally accepted views of the 'cruelty of nature,' the 'struggle for existence,' and so forth can scarcely be imagined. Yet such ideas, because of their emotional content, are really anthropomorphisms. For the cat, unlike the kind of human being who would act out of conscious cruelty, is incapable of enjoying its victim's fear. When we free ourselves from emotional clichés and begin to view nature in an unbiased way, the truth becomes apparent to us: the cat and mouse complement one another, not only physiologically, but even on a psychological, or soul, level. Each bestows a benefit upon the other. The cat satisfies its urge to hunt and its hunger, and the mouse is permitted to die."

What about when an ungulate, like a zebra or a wildebeest, is killed by a predator? In that case, says Schad, death is not accepted with such easy equanimity. "For the ungulate," writes Schad, "the physical organism is the most important aspect of life, and it therefore parts with its body reluctantly." But that does not mean that a hoofed mammal brought down by a lion or a cheetah experiences death in a purely negative manner. "Even when a large deeply incarnated ungulate is killed by a carnivore," Schad writes, "its death is not in fact accompanied by the terrible pain we humans usually ascribe to it."

It seems this exemption from the terror one would naturally associate with being devoured by a wild beast can extend, sometimes, even to humans. The British explorer David Livingstone experienced something remarkably similar when he was attacked by a wild lion in Africa. "Growling horribly close to my ear," Livingstone wrote, "he shook me as a terrier dog does a rat. The shock produced a stupor similar to that which seems to be felt by a mouse after the first shake of the cat. It caused a sort of dreaminess, in which there was no sense of pain nor feeling of terror, though I was quite conscious of all that was happening. It was like what patients partially under the influence of chloroform describe, who see all the operation, but feel not the knife. This singular condition was not the result of any mental process. The shake annihilated fear, and allowed no sense of horror even at the sight of the beast."

With their emphasis on the physical body as a kind of vehicle or an outfit that can be worn loosely or tightly and discarded with either joy or reluctance, Schad's descriptions of the animal soul echo the beliefs of the earth's primordial peoples—so much so that one can't help but wonder at the consistency, unity, and coherence of this general perspective. Yes, both parties assert, animals do have souls. But no, their souls are not exactly the same as ours. That the views of the spiritual scientist and of the primitive overlap so significantly gives still more credence to Henry Beston's assertion that animals "are not brethren, they are not underlings; they are other nations, caught with ourselves in the net of life and time, fellow prisoners of the splendor and travail of the earth."

Apart, Yet Not Apart

The viewpoint of spiritual scientists like Schad also gives further weight to that universal intuition that humans occupy, if not a superior, then a decidedly special place in the Great Chain of Being. Above the animals and below the angels, we are like a summary statement of all creation, able (at least potentially) to communicate both with the animal and the spiritual levels of creation with equal facility.

"A human being," writes Schad, "is not only 'Man'; he is also a physical being and therefore bears the world of matter within him. He lives and grows and thus shares certain qualities with the plants; and his emotional, or soul, life connects him with the animals. Only the fourth part of his nature, in which his soul participates in the world of spirit, forms his purely human essence. All the realms of nature are present within man and in him they coexist harmoniously. In man, therefore, we can observe in microcosm how the kingdoms of nature are related to form a whole outside man."

This picture of the human role in nature is very close to that of Aristotle and the logic-happy churchmen like Augustine, and Aquinas who followed him. But it is also, of course, quite different, in that it allows humans to stand "above" animals on the Chain of Being without thereby cutting animal creation off from its higher levels. In the metaphysical world-picture outlined by Schad, Goethe, Corbin's Islamic philosophers, and the more sympathetic voices from the Christian tradition, heaven is a place where all of nature is allowed to enter. The heavenly landscapes described by Islamic mystical speculation are populated not only by deer and birds but by trees, streams, and rocks as well, and however literally we choose to read these descriptions, their philosophical meaning is crystal clear: all material creation possesses a spiritual nature, and this fact vouchsafes that creation *in its entirety* will be invited into the world above.

All this is summed up admirably by Seyyed Hossein Nasr, one of the most accomplished interpreters of Islam to the modern world. In his book *Man and Nature,* Nasr writes: "Man stands in fact between the spiritual and material creations and partakes of the nature of both. In him the whole creation is contained in an essential rather than a material or substantial sense. Man is created in the image of God, yet as an animal, so that from one side the spiritual world is reflected in him and from the other the animal world. His destiny is inextricably tied to both the spiritual and natural worlds. This is why the apokatastasis or the final restoration means the passage of spiritualized nature to God and the restoration of all things including animals and trees."

As beings made in God's image, humans sum up all of creation in a manner that sets us above and apart from the rest of animal creation. But our special position does not, or at least should not, cut us off from the animal kingdom. Instead, it should only unite us to it all the more deeply, for it places upon us a unique responsibility. As the creature that sums up all creation, and as the only creature that can consciously witness, understand, and honor that creation in all its variety, we have the job on earth to act as the Hebrew Bible originally intended when it said that we hold "dominion" over the natural world. Understood rightly, this is not a dominion of brutal mastery but of compassion, steward-ship, and openness to the essential mystery and integrity that all animals embody. "Stewardship" is, by the way, an overused word in books describing our relationship to and responsibilities toward animals, but it's a good one all the same, perhaps espe-cially as it derives, originally, from "sty ward"—that is, a man whose job it was to watch over and guard an enclosure of pigs.

The Return of the Beasts

One can become reconciled to the horrors of history if one cherishes the great hope of a resurrection of all who have lived and are living, of every creature who has suffered and rejoiced.

—*Nicholas Berdyaev (1874–1948)*

Valentine

The dog [is] the animal most passionately drawn and attached to the human element, as a symbol of the aspiration of animals toward union with human nature.

—*Valentin Tomberg (1900–1973)*

All through the spring of 2005, I received almost daily cards and letters responding to my pets-in-heaven piece. I was still receiving them in June, when my wife Rebecca's and my aging toy poodle, Valentine, grew ill. We had originally taken Valentine into our home some eight years previously, after it became apparent that he was too much for my elderly mother to look after. Val, as we came to call him, had started his life as a show dog. I was with my mother the day (Valentine's Day, as it happened) that he arrived at her house, and from the moment she pulled him from his crate I could see that those years in the spotlight had left their mark. Val wasn't just obedient—he was downright robotic.

When he sat, he did so the way I imagined a show dog would—head up, eyes straight ahead. When he walked, he walked the way I figured a show dog would as well: like a tiny French soldier on parade.

He even had a robotic name, written atop his long and impressive pedigree: Chip 5716. "What an awful name!" My mother had exclaimed. Then, in honor of the day of his arrival, she gave him his new one.

I have to say that when Rebecca first suggested that we take care of Valentine, I wasn't too keen on the idea. While I liked Val, I had never envisioned myself as a poodle—especially a *toy* poodle—owner. As a kid, I'd always imagined owning a big, romantic, wolflike dog: the kind that showed up in the stories of Jack London and Ernest Thompson Seton. With his slender, diminutive frame and his delicate ways, Val put me more in mind of a miniature deer than a dog, and when he struck certain poses he reminded me of a hornless version of the unicorn in the famous medieval Unicorn Tapestries in which the mythical beast, chased through a magical wood by a group of hounds and huntsmen, is a symbol of the dying god, perishing at the hands of the uncaring world.

Val took well to his new post-dog-show lifestyle with my mother, and by the time Rebecca and I brought him into our apartment he had learned how—for moments at least—actually to have a little fun. Though he still sat stock-still most of the time and usually had the same anxious, ready-to-please expression on his face that he'd come out of the crate wearing, he also gave in, every now and then, to short, tenuous, but oddly heroic moments of playfulness: moments when, in spite of all the drilling he had received, he would let down his guard and allow his true dog personality, bottled up for so long, to emerge.

One weekend a month or so after we got Valentine, we took him and our Schipperke, Mercury, out into the country.

"Should we let him off the leash?" Rebecca asked me.

"Why not?" I said. "He'll probably just stand at attention."

But he didn't. With his leash off and a big field of grass in front of him, Val took off like a rocket. For ten straight minutes he raced back and forth, zooming in at Mercury, then tearing away again like a jet fighter harassing a sluggish navy cruiser. Finally, chest heaving and tongue lolling, he collapsed on the ground—a thoroughly relaxed, thoroughly exhausted, thoroughly happy dog. All those years at attention hadn't killed his plucky little spirit after all.

But there was something else those years hadn't killed as well. For the first time, watching him race around on that green field, I caught a glimpse of what—or *who*—Valentine really was. From the days of the great Paleolithic hunt, down through the invention of agriculture and the growth of villages, then towns, then cities across the face of the earth, animals had accompanied us as we grew and changed in our relation to the world. They, or rather some of them, changed too, abandoning their pure wildness and taking on, in varying degrees, the burdens and benefits of human culture. In that bargain animals had both lost and gained, as we humans had as well. The human-animal relationship brought humans a number of woes, mostly in the form of diseases arising from our close contact with them. But the benefits had far outnumbered the drawbacks, and it was in fact really thanks to animals that we *became* truly human to begin with.

The history of humans and animals is so tightly interwoven that it is impossible to conceive of our world without them. What did animals receive as their part of this bargain? Food and shelter, certainly, but also pain: the pain of labor, of confinement, and perhaps most of all the pain of manipulation: of transformation, at the hands of humans, into creatures they had not originally been.

It would have been hard to find a more vivid embodiment of this fact than Valentine. With his tiny size, fragile constitution, and silly haircut, Val was as pure a product of human manipulation of the natural world as you could hope to find. But he was still, at heart, a dog: a member of that branch of the *Canis* family that, thirty thousand years ago, had come into the human house or *domus* (though at that time the only domiciles on earth were tents and caves). As such, he still retained a wild and supremely mysterious spark: one that all those years of meddling on our part had failed to touch. As the wilderness shrank from an engulfing enormity to small islands of green, we took animals out of that wilderness and into our homes, so that it became their job, as pets, to carry that lost, original wild world inside them. Like Angus, Valentine was an unofficial representative of something sacred and lost—and in those sudden wild bursts of speed that he allowed himself at times to indulge in, I caught sight of that lost sacred essence once more.

By the fall of 2004 Valentine had, along with Mercury, grown a small white beard. He'd also left his days of lightning-fast running behind, and as Christmas approached it became apparent to Rebecca and me that his health was deteriorating. He spent most of the day curled up in his bed, and I sometimes had to carry him down to the street for his walks.

Our vet told us she wasn't sure what was wrong, but prescribed a course of steroids. The pills put Val back on his feet for a few months, but by late spring it was clear that their effectiveness was wearing off. Early on the morning of July 4, while we were vacationing on Long Island, Valentine wasn't able to get up for his morning walk. I carried him outside and put him down on the grass, but his legs gave way immediately. Emitting a little yelp of pain, he fell onto his side, chest heaving in the way it had back in the days when he would race happily around the yard.

Rebecca found an emergency veterinary clinic that was open despite the holiday, and we rushed him over. The doctors there told us what we already knew: Valentine was in a great deal of discomfort, and the kindest thing to do would be to have him put to sleep.

The vets placed Valentine on an operating table and inserted a needle into his leg just above his paw. Rebecca and I each carefully placed a hand on Valentine's ribcage, and I thought back to the day I'd first seen him emerge from his crate at my mother's. In spite of all his years as a show dog, in spite of the daunting genetic and behavioral load of human manipulation he demonstrated in every aspect of his body and behavior, Valentine had been not just our pet but a link to another, older world. He, like all companion animals, was a reminder that all of us at heart are spirits in a material world, and that no matter what the material world does to us, we retain in our essence a spark of that pure, original place from which both humans and animals once came.

A Show of Fireworks

This would be a good place for me to say that as the shot was administered and Val left his body, I saw a blue etheric puff of smoke above him, or that his spirit came to me later in a dream and I saw him racing happily across the green fields of the world above this one: the heavenly earth that, in their different ways, the shamans of prehistory, the sages of medieval Islam, the spiritualists and spiritual scientists of more recent times, and the readers of *Guideposts* had all helped me to understand might just be a real place after all.

Rebecca actually did have a very vivid dream of Valentine just a few days after his death, and a couple of times, back in our apartment, I had double-take moments when I thought I saw Val out of the corner of my eye, much in the way that I'd seen those shadow apparitions of Angus back in San Diego. But what I remember best about Val's death is what happened that night on the way back to Manhattan. Tied up in traffic on the Long Island Expressway just outside the city, we found ourselves with a perfect—if accidental—view of the Fourth of July fireworks show on the East River. Watching the single, solitary flares corkscrew up into the night sky one after the other, it occurred to me what a clear—what an *obvious*—symbol fireworks are for the postmortem soul. Each of us, say the teachings of the world's soul traditions, possesses a larger self or identity: one of which we experience only tiny hints and flashes while down here on earth, but that rises and transforms, at death, into something larger, stranger, and better than we could ever imagine. Animals like Valentine and Angus, and all the others that readers of my

Guideposts story had written to tell me about, were never for a moment *just* earthly beings, and when viewed with that in mind, their deaths became something larger, stranger, and altogether better, too.

The Duty of Friendship

One of the most unusual letters I got for my *Guideposts* story came from one of the practicing veterinarians who wrote in—a woman named Carol Galka-Agnew. Accompanying it was a stapled treatise of Carol's thoughts on the animal soul that she had written called "God's Covenant with the Animal Kingdom."

In large part, her story was a familiar one. "For years," Carol wrote in it, "I had searched for the answer to the question of whether animals went to heaven when they died. I asked every religious leader I could find; and the most common answer I received was that animals don't even have intelligence, let alone souls. I was devastated. In fact, I almost gave up my career in veterinary medicine."

Carol's pain over this question was typical of that expressed in so many of the letters I received. But because she was a vet, dealing with an endless number of animals in real-life distress every day, I found her story especially affecting.

"I *had* to know," she wrote, "that God made provision for animals in his eternal plan. I could not face one more broken-hearted client grieving the loss of their pet without having an assurance for them that God loves the animals he has created even more than we do."

Eventually, Carol came, through looking into herself and

reading the Bible with this question in mind, to believe that animals did have souls, and that they did indeed matter to God. In a sense, Carol, like so many of the people who wrote to me about my piece, already knew the answer to her question. She just had to realize that she knew it.

But her document also raised, and answered, another important question for me: a question centering on the meaning of the word *friendship*. As we saw in the first half of this book, the history of the animal-human relationship is one in which humans and animals began as separate nations that lived apart from each other after falling away from a state of unity for which both sides were homesick. But that relationship changed over time. People, as they got ever more efficient at living on earth and making use of its resources, stopped seeing animals as fellow nations fallen from a common country above, and started looking at them as secondary beings: creatures that existed in large part for human convenience and pleasure rather than for their own sakes.

So it stayed for a time. A very long time in fact. But gradually a new human-animal relationship took over: one that is still in the process of unfolding today, and that Carol witnessed every day in her veterinary practice. The more estranged people became from the natural world beyond the borders of civilization, the more important pets became for them. Animal companions were no longer just diverting or comforting, they were *necessary*. As companion animals have become ever more vital to modern life (to the point it has reached today when a city like New York can sometimes seem, early on a weekday morning, like a city of dogs as much as it is of people), humans and animals have found themselves in an odd situation. The animal-human relationship these days is a little like that between cells and mitochondria. Eons ago, mitochondria were separate entities, useful but not essential to the unicellular organisms with which they interacted. But over time, mitochondria began to take up residence within the walls of cells, doing work for them that both the mitochondria and the cell that housed it benefited from. Then, finally, the mitochondria simply became a permanent part of the cell itself.

So it is with our more intimate companion animals these days. Having stepped so thoroughly inside the world we humans have made, these animals are no longer really visitors from the wilderness at all, but close to full-fledged members of our human world. They have become our companions in the deepest sense of the word, and the result is that we are no longer able to look at them half with the affection of a friend and half with the disregard of an owner (like John Berger's peasant who was fond of his pig and was also happy to salt away its meat), but *entirely* as friends. It's because our companion animals have stepped, for better or worse, so completely aboard the ship of human culture with us that so many people now feel so urgently compelled to understand, in a spiritual sense, *just what these creatures are.* Are they true soul beings like we are? And if they are, how best should we relate to them?

This realization that animals are beings with a genuine interior existence can be as painful as it is powerful. Year after year as a vet, Carol witnessed animal suffering every day, and the more she saw of animals, the more she came to see them not as creatures of pure conditioning and instinct, but as beings who think and make profound decisions about the way they relate to humans. "Dogs," she writes, "do not automatically give unconditional love. But they do show their love and acceptance of people unconditionally once they have made the decision to give their love to someone. I have seen many, many animals come into my clinic with an obvious desire *not* to leave again. When animals are treated with kindness, respect and dignity, they do not willingly return to a situation where they are considered to be valueless 'property.' When an animal is considered a disposable possession and there is no emotional bond between the person and the animal, the animal does *not* have unconditional love for that person. The animal may be perpetually hopeful that the person will enter into a covenant bond with the animal. But until that bond is forged, until that covenant is agreed upon, I assure you that animals will gladly switch allegiance to the first person that treats them with dignity, gives the love they deserve and values the animal as an individual being."

Carol speaks not as a softhearted sentimentalist who projects human feelings onto animals without having any real knowledge of what makes them tick, but as a professional who deals with the real-life complexities of animal behavior every day. "Please do not think," she writes, "that I am saying that animals and humans are the same. It's precisely because they are *not* human that animals are so very special. They are different from humans in certain respects, but created by God the same way we were."

"Friendship," wrote C. S. Lewis, "is unnecessary, like philosophy, like art, like the universe itself (for God did not need to create). It has no survival value; rather it is one of those things which give value to survival." But is this always true? In the case of humans and animals, friendship seems—in these days of our ever-increasing alienation from nature—very necessary indeed.

The Man Beneath the Tree

Working at *Guideposts*, it was easy to get swallowed up in questions about Western religion, and to forget about the question of how Eastern faiths fit into the general picture of the earth above the earth, and the human and animal souls that dwell there. After I started thinking a lot about the animal soul again, I would find myself returning, now and then, to the question of whether there was a way of envisioning the soul life of animals in a way that really and truly included the spiritual traditions of *both* East and West.

To my mind, the chief stumbling block to this—and the factor that made me lean ever more in the direction of the Western rather than the Eastern faith traditions—continued to be the way Eastern religions seemed so often to dismiss the issue of personality. As we saw earlier, that Eastern faiths don't place great stock in animals as enduring spiritual personalities isn't really all that surprising, considering that they typically have the same attitude toward human beings. What matters for Eastern religions is union with the Absolute: an Absolute that so completely transcends the particularities of phenomenal existence that questions of the survival of personality are largely beside the point. Worrying about the fate of the individual personality, for the East, is like fussing about the fate of the champagne bottle at the christening of a ship. What matters is precisely the *transcendence* of personality, and of all the endless worries, woes, fears, and delusions that it brings along with it.

Western religions, on the other hand, tend to go in the exact opposite direction, envisioning the absolute as a God who is not only personal but who also profoundly cherishes the specificity in all that he creates—a God who is *so* personal that, in Judaism, Christianity, and Islam, he is often spoken of as if he were literally a person himself. Nonhuman creation often gets shut out of the picture in Western religion, but in those places where it isn't, the result is a spirituality that includes and embraces the specificity of animal creation—and the absolutely unique personality of each dog or cat—in a way that to my mind the Eastern religions simply don't.

But if both East and West have their significant strengths and equally significant weaknesses in their approach to animal creation, beyond those strengths and weaknesses there is a place where East and West meet, and meet decisively. And a glimpse of that place can be found by returning to that image of the man beneath the tree that Nicky described to me on that squirrel-filled spring day in the park.

One day, cleaning some books out of the sun porch in our apartment, I stumbled across my stepdaughter Mara's old copy of *The World of Pooh*, a book that combined the two original Pooh books *Winnie the Pooh* and *The House at Pooh Corner*. I hadn't taken a look at the Pooh stories in many a year, and flipping through the pages released an instant flood of nostalgia. My mother had read both books to me as a child during a winter we spent in Fort Myers, Florida. Remembering the sadness— or, more specifically, the happy-sadness—that I'd felt on the day when my mother and I had finished the last of the stories, I turned to the final chapter of *The House at Pooh Corner*: "In Which Christopher Robin and Pooh Come to an Enchanted Place, and We Leave Them There."

"Christopher Robin," the chapter began, "was going away. Nobody knew why he was going; nobody knew where he was going; indeed, nobody even knew why he knew that Christopher Robin *was* going away. But somehow or other everybody in the Forest felt that it was happening at last."

The lines pulled me in and I kept going, reading about how all the animals of the Hundred-Acre Wood decide to send Christopher Robin off by composing a signed poem in honor of him. Then, turning another page, my eye fell on one of E. H. Shepard's big two-page black-and-white illustrations. The second I saw it, I remembered how long I'd stared at it back when my mother had first read me the book, so many years ago. In it, Christopher Robin stands beneath the generous, spreading branches of a tree. The tree is not just any tree, however, but the one in which, according to the fanciful logic of the Pooh stories, Christopher Robin lives. There is a door in the tree, and looking at it, I remembered how wonderful I'd thought it would be to be able to live in such a structure myself: to enter the trunk and climb up, up, and up, into the branches of the world above.

Christopher Robin is not pictured alone beneath this tree. Gathered before him are the creatures of the Hundred-Acre Wood: Eeyore, Piglet, Rabbit, Pooh, Kanga, Roo, Owl, Tigger, and even a smattering of the beetles and bugs that we are told constitute Rabbit's extensive collection of friends and relations. Looking at that picture, the whole spiritual history of humans and animals suddenly spread itself out before me: not just the archaic picture, not just the more modern Western picture, and not just the Eastern picture either, but . . . the *whole* picture. The Jesus of the Sermon on the Mount, who blessed the lilies of the field and the birds of the air and who, like Christopher Robin, was at home in the innocent world of the beasts but who could also navigate the fallen world of humanity out beyond it, was present there. So, too, was the Adam of Genesis in the days before the Fall, naming each of Eden's animals in its turn after God created them, just as Christopher Robin gave names to all of his animal friends. Artemis, the Greek goddess of woods and wilderness, was there, as was Orpheus, the charmer of the beasts. And the East's great spiritual figures were present in the picture as well. Lao Tzu was there. So, too, was Rama, the blue-skinned god of popular Hindu belief who loved all the beasts of the forest, and whose closest and most loyal companion was the monkey god Hanuman. And so, too, of course, was the Buddha, seated rapt in meditation beneath the Bodhi tree, dead set on achieving spiritual liberation for every last cat, dog, butterfly, and beetle in the universe.

But someone else was present in that illustration, too. Someone who contained all of those other figures, and who through his constant presence in the spiritual traditions of both the East *and* the West was the key to the best and truest parts of what all of those traditions had had to say about the fate of the animal soul over the centuries.

The Master of Animals. That universal, ageless, all-encompassing figure who joined the sundered worlds of earth and heaven and of beasts and men: he was right there, in that children's book about a boy and a stuffed bear, and the perfect world of human and nonhuman harmony they created together.

The Meeting-Place of All Creation

The Master of Animals could take on all kinds of animal attributes, but in both the East and the West he was first and foremost a human being. He appeared so consistently as a human because even in the earliest times it was understood that we humans, separate and strange in comparison to all the other creatures of the world though we may be, are uniquely *necessary* beings as well. Writing about the Great Chain of Being, the Eastern Orthodox philosopher Philip Sherrard says that "man possesses, in various degrees of actualization, bodily forms that are spiritual, psychic and material, together with all the various interconnecting forms that link these levels one with another. He thus epitomizes in his own being the whole Platonic hierarchy of forms, or images, stretching from heaven to earth." In other words, we humans have been created to do more than simply comprehend the world, and the hierarchical levels of matter and spirit that make it up. We humans, created uniquely in the image of the divine, *are* that multilevel world, containing the whole hierarchy of earthly and spiritual creation within ourselves.

"All things in creation," writes Sherrard, "have their meeting-place in man, and man is potentially all things." Therefore, the task of humankind is to see nature as "part of his own subjectivity, as the living garment of his own inner being. . . . It is only through man fulfilling his role as mediator between God and the world that the world itself can fulfill its destiny and be transfigured in the light and presence of God."

That's why, from the Buddha to Jesus to Saint Francis to

Ramakrishna to Dr. Dolittle, one of the most powerful and consistent ways of presenting the holy man (or woman) is by picturing him or her surrounded by animals and sitting beneath the branches of the cosmic tree. We humans, say the sages of both East and West, do more than just dwell (as Christopher Robin managed to do literally) at the juncture of the natural and the supernatural worlds. We *are* that juncture. Lower than the angels yet higher than the beasts (though perhaps, as Henry Beston suggested, less complete and perfect than either group), we are creatures strangely and uniquely clumsy and out of place in the world. From angels to antelopes, the creatures both above and beneath us on the great hierarchy of being all seem to know what they are doing much better than we do. And yet in spite of this—in spite of our being such odd (and often dangerous and destructive) additions to the tree of life—we have something that no other being, be it animal or angel, has. Containing all the worlds of heaven and earth within ourselves, it is we and we alone who, in the wake of the Fall out of Eden, hold the keys back into it. That's why Lao Tzu, despite his feelings about the superiority of untouched nature to most of what passes for human culture on the earth, made such a point, in his little manual of wisdom, of emphasizing how necessary we humans are to creation all the same.

One day after I'd started writing a fair number of animal-related pieces in *Guideposts*, I got a letter from a gentleman named Rich. An antiques dealer in upstate New York, Rich wanted to share a story with me about something that had happened to him recently while walking in the woods behind his house.

"I came upon a small rabbit lying in the middle of the trail," Rich wrote. "It had been mauled by some other animal, a cat or perhaps a hawk, and was very close to death. Its eyes were wide, its little chest heaved up and down. I knew I couldn't do anything for the rabbit, but somehow I couldn't just leave it there either. So I sat down next to it and just kind of kept it company for its last few minutes of life."

The rabbit finally died, and Rich got up and went on with his walk. But—as certain encounters with animals will do—the moment stayed with him. It meant something to him—something he knew was important, even if he couldn't figure out exactly what that something was. "I don't really know why I'm telling you this," Rich wrote. "Somehow or other, I just figured you'd understand."

Rich was right. In fact, his story of sitting down beneath the trees of that forest to keep a dying rabbit company said more to me than he could ever have imagined. Because I knew that Rich hadn't really been alone with that rabbit beneath those trees. Someone else was with him, someone who had gone by many names since the dawn of life on earth, disappearing and coming back into view again countless times in the history of both the East and the West; someone who was every bit as present—and important—in our world today as he had ever been before.

Over the Fence

This book started with a meeting: one that took place between me and a dog I named Penny, on a morning on the Yucatán Peninsula sometime in the fall of 1974. And just as I could think of no better place to start this book, there seems no better place to end it, either.

Who or what, I asked at the beginning of this book, *was* Penny in the end? Was she anything at all? Was there something of her that remained after the breath left her body and she transformed from a living being—a *nephesh chaya*—into what, at least to earthly eyes, was a simple, small, pathetic bundle of bones, fur, and flesh?

Having traveled the length of this book, we can add another question to this list. Spiritually speaking, if humans are in fact different from animals, and if animals somehow sense this fact, what consequences does this have in the real world?

Few people alert to animal life and animal suffering are unfamiliar with the feeling one gets when, looking at a dog like Penny or a rabbit like the one Rich encountered in the woods, one realizes that one wants to help, but simply can't. How, we ask ourselves, can we live with our frequent powerlessness in the face of the ugly realities of life in the physical world? And what kind of world is it in which such a question needs to be asked in the first place?

The answer—not unanimous but very close to it—given by the spiritual traditions of the world is that the kind of world we live in is the *fallen* kind. Even in the Eastern faiths, where the Judeo-Christian concept of the Fall isn't present, there is often the powerful feeling that the world as we experience it is deeply off kilter somehow. Even traditions like Zen Buddhism that stress total and unquestioning acceptance of the world just as it is betray, by their very emphasis on this discipline, their belief that accepting the world just as we find it is a very tough feat indeed.

So given that—as the sages of both the East and the West tell us—there is something very seriously wrong with things, and that animal suffering is one of the prime ways in which this basic off-kilter-ness of the world presents itself . . . *what do we do about it?* That is, what do we do in those situations where action is impossible, and we are forced to simply witness the cruelty and profound unfairness of physical life toward the rest of animal creation?

One way to answer this is by asking what, in a perfect world, we would desire for all the suffering creatures we encounter in life. What, to go back to Penny once again, would I have wanted for her? If I had suddenly found myself living in a world where anything was possible and I could choose any fate for Penny that I wanted, what fate *would* I have chosen?

The answer to that is easy: I would have chosen to set her free. Free not just from the chicken-wire fence that closed her in, but free from the physical world itself; free from everything confining, everything negative, and everything destructive to the core of pure innocence and goodness that I saw so clearly in her eyes.

"Man can be truly human," writes Philip Sherrard, "only when he is mindful of his theriomorphic nature. When he ignores the divine in himself and in other existences he becomes sub-human."

Theriomorphic means capable of transforming into a god: capable of divine life. Not only humans, according to the traditional view—the great tradition that stretches back to the Paleolithic, embraces both East and West, and is the oldest and truest map of the universe and the place of the human and animal spirit within it that we have—are potentially divine, but all of nature is as well. Not only are humans destined to enjoy a life in the world of spirit that preceded the birth of the physical universe and that will survive its death, but it is precisely the job of humans to lead all of physical creation back into that world of spirit as well.

Do animals go to heaven? After a lot of thinking on the matter, I am convinced that they do. But animals don't simply go to heaven along with us. They go to heaven *because* of us. We not only meet on the Rainbow Bridge with the animals we love. Seen in a certain light, it is we ourselves who *are* that bridge. And if ever we should forget that fact, a glance into the eyes of an animal is all we need to remember it.

A Place at the Table

Religious traditions that speak in detail of what will happen when the world of matter is rescued and returned to the world of spirit often use the metaphor of a giant feast or party. The most important question to ask about any party, earthly or heavenly, is, Who is invited? Will humans alone be present at the great feast that celebrates the reunion of the earthly and the spiritual worlds, or will animals (as they are in certain medieval biblical illustrations of the millennial feast) be there too?

Many voices from the world's most vocal and influential spiritual traditions have maintained very firmly that there will be no dogs or cats—or llamas or lemurs or ostriches or giraffes—present at that feast. Not only will humans and humans alone be present, those voices often say, but only a very select number of those humans to boot: those who have embraced a certain creed or doctrine, or those who have been born into a certain caste or high social station. For the rest, there is either perdition or simple nonexistence.

But that's not what the wiser voices say. It's not what Church Fathers like Clement or Origen or Gregory of Nyssa said. Nor is it what Saint Paul or Saint Francis or the mystics of Islam or Lao Tzu or Chuang Tzu or the Buddha or the Hindu sage Nagarjuna or Gandhi said, either. East or West, when the most inclusive, wise, and humane voices speak of a resolution of the terrible conflict between the world as it is and the world as it should be, all of human and nonhuman creation is always given a place at the table.

Is all this naïve? Absolutely. The Indo-European root of the word *naïve* is *gn*—the same root that gives us the Greek word *gnosis* and the English word *knowledge*. Naïveté, in other words, originally connoted not ignorance but knowledge: the kind of knowledge that all of us possessed before the Fall. The kind of knowledge that knows that in spite of all the horror and pain of the world, in the end all shall be well.

In his autobiography, the twentieth-century Russian philosopher Nicholas Berdyaev describes the illness and death of his beloved cat, Muri. "I experienced Muri's suffering before his death," Berdyaev writes, "as the suffering of all creation. Through him I felt myself united to the whole of creation awaiting deliverance. . . . I very rarely weep, but when Muri died, I wept bitterly. And the death of such a charming one of God's creatures was for me the experience of death in general. I demand for myself eternal life with Muri."

Berdyaev, though not as widely read today as he was fifty

or sixty years ago, is considered by some to have been one of the most profound and penetrating philosophical minds of the twentieth century. His early masterpiece *The Meaning of the Creative Act* has been hailed as one of the greatest meditations on the metaphysical underpinnings of the human imagination ever written. No one would deny that Berdyaev was possessed of a truly formidable intellect. Yet when it came to his feelings upon the death of his cat, he sounds practically indistinguishable from the ranchers, corn farmers, and retired grandmothers who wrote in about my *Guideposts* pets-in-heaven piece.

What are we called upon to do when we see a suffering animal that we can't help, or when we watch a beloved pet come to the end of its life before our eyes? Paradoxical as it may seem, what we are called on to do is simply to *believe.* Believe the voice within us that assures us that no matter what certain scientists or clergy people or whoever else might have to say to the contrary, the soul of that departing animal is real: every bit as real as our own soul, and different only in its specific character and capacity—the varied charms and faults and glories and limitations that go to making it specifically and unrepeatably *itself* and not another. The tug in our hearts when we feel compassion for an animal is actually the whole invisible hierarchical world pulling at us—pulling and urging us to remember that it is out there, whether we can see it or not, and that it holds a place within it for every living creature.

Augustine and Aquinas, though they went decidedly and disastrously overboard in their insistence that the possession of reason was necessary for salvation, weren't entirely wrong in their belief that humans and animals are different. As should be apparent by now, something does indeed separate us from them, but that something has less to do with reason or logic than with another attribute: one that the word *logic* itself derives from. That word is *Logos.*

Logos is Greek for "word," but in pre-Christian Greek philosophy, and in the later Christian philosophies that made use of that philosophy, it meant much more than that. In a nutshell, it meant the essence of the divine: the part of God that did not stay with God at the creation of the world, but that traveled down into the world and dwelt there.

Humans, the traditional teachings maintain, manifest the Logos more perfectly than any other being. But what's important is that though other creatures can't give voice to the Logos with the perfection that humans do, that doesn't mean they don't have a share in it all the same.

"We cannot argue," wrote the nineteenth-century bishop Stanley Butler, "from the reason of the thing that death is the destruction of living agents. Neither can we find anything in the whole analogy of nature to afford us even the slightest presumption that animals ever lose their living powers; much less, if it were possible, that they lose them by death. The immortality of brutes does not necessarily imply that they are endowed with any latent capacities of a rational or moral nature. The economy of the universe might require that there should be immortal creatures without any capacities of this kind."

In other words, even if animals don't manifest the Logos or essence of the divine in the form of conscious rational ability in the way that humans can, this does not necessarily bar them from participation in the immortality of the divine life that so many traditions, from the archaic to the modern, promise awaits us. That's why Saint Francis could address all animals as if they were his brothers without fear of going against the truth he found in the scriptures, and it's why so many Eastern saints and holy people could treat animals as if they were their brethren as well.

As if they were their brethren . . . Animals, said Henry Beston in the quote from *The Outermost House* with which we began this book, are not our brethren—and he was right. Animals *are* different from us, but they are different in a way that doesn't separate us from them so much as it unites us in a common task and a common future. Animals are individuals. If every rabbit is Rabbit, if it is both an individual and a manifestation, at the same time, of its heavenly archetype, so all other animals are as well. But it takes little effort to see that there is a *scale* of individuality at work here: that each chimpanzee or gray whale is more uniquely itself than, say, each Atlantic salmon or green tree frog or (if we want to keep going) each fruit fly or paramecium. And it is not, I think, an insult to the animal community to suggest that we humans, if not the only beings on earth that are each born unique, nonetheless manifest this trait most profoundly and consequentially. We humans are, in a sense, the champions of individuality—a belief that the sages of Islam expressed by stating that each individual human being is in itself its own species.

That's why animals—like Moose the Manatee and Little Bit the black bear—so often seem to become *more* individual, more distinct from their fellows, when they spend time with humans. If heaven is above all a place that is personal, then at our best we humans inspire animals to move ever closer to that heaven by allowing them to become ever more themselves in our presence. And they, in turn, do the same for us.

And what's most important of all to realize is that we do this even when we see an animal only for a second. Outrageous as it sounds, that single moment of connection I enjoyed with Penny—that instant when I looked her in the eyes and saw her for the soul being she truly was—actually made a difference in her life. For if it is the job of humans to manifest the divine—the Logos that informs every creature upon the earth to one degree or another—in a more complete and consequential manner than any other earthly creature can, it is not in order to block access on the part of those creatures to the divine, but to connect them to it all the more fully and completely.

By meeting Penny's hopeful glance that day, I gave her a glimpse of the bridge: the bridge that connects this world to the world to come, and that every last creature on earth is destined, some way and somehow, to cross. In doing so, even though I could not reach over that crummy chicken-wire fence, take her in my arms, and set Penny free from the world she was caught in, I *did* set her free all the same. In seeing Penny for the soul being that she in truth was, I joined forces with the Master of Animals him/herself in the great task of picking up all creation, and bringing it back over into paradise.

ACKNOWLEDGMENTS

Thanks to all of the following: Jonathan Merkh (for getting me started), Rebecca Weiner (for helping me along), Keren Baltzer (for doing same), Macklin Trimnell and Jed Hershon at Atlantic Books in Brooklyn (for running one of the greater New York area's last good used bookstores), Kate Farrell (for her ideas, insights, and enormous encouragement), Philip Zaleski (for same), Michael Mountain, Bokara Legendre, Leeza Mangaldas, Nicholas Vreeland (for generously putting me up during a stretch of the writing), Godfrey Cheshire, Mara Lieber, Thomas Grady, Clayton Carlson, Michael Loughran, Robin Ray (for enormous help and general toleration), Stuart Ray (for same times two), Christie Ray Robb, Steve Robb, Oliver Ray, Mitch Horowitz (for his friendship and encouragement), Lucinda Bartley at the Crown Publishing Group (for her fantastic and tireless editing), Rachel Klayman, also at Crown (for thinking, perhaps misguidedly, that I'm generally worthwhile), my altogether excellent agent Gail Ross along with Howard Yoon, Jennifer Manguera, and Anna Sproul (for all their help at every station of the way), Clayton and Caryl Eshleman, Edward Grinnan and Rick Hamlin at *Guideposts*, Steve Bendich, Tonne Goodman, Sarah Golden (for Angus and all that he wrought), Karl Taro Greenfeld, David Wade Smith (for his careful copyediting), Topher Davis, Richard Ryan, Lisa Train, Heather Higgins, and last but not least Colleen Hughes, editor of *Angels on Earth* magazine, where I have learned so much about making complicated things simple without completely messing them up along the way.

A NOTE ON SOURCES

Strangely enough, histories of the way humans have perceived animals over the centuries are few and generally quite daunting (Francis Kling- ender's *Animals in Art and Thought to the End of the Middle Ages* [MIT Press, 1971], for example, is full of interesting material but is extremely large, hard to come by, and—as the title admits—only takes one up to the Middle Ages). One of the best overall views of the way humans have looked at and treated animals, however, is also one of the shortest. Linda Kalof's *Looking at Animals in Human History* (Reaktion Books, 2007) manages to tell the essentials of the story (or at least the West- ern side of it) in under two hundred very clearly written pages. The book's bibliography is also a treasure trove of references to other useful works. Also extremely worthwhile is *The Animals Reader: The Essen- tial Classic and Contemporary Writings* (Berg Publishers, 2007), edited by Kalof and Amy Fitzgerald. Richard W. Bulliet's *Hunters, Herders, and Hamburgers: The Past and Future of Human-Animal Relationships* (Columbia University Press, 2005) is an academic but readable—and often provocative—tour of the animal-human relationship from pre- history to the present, with an emphasis on the unprecedented distance that now separates us from the animals whose lives and bodies all of us, to some degree, rely on for our own existence. The book provided me with an especially large number of facts and insights that were crucial in writing this book. Matt Cartmill's *A View to a Death in the Morning: Hunting and Nature Through History* (Harvard University Press, 1996) is a survey of what hunting has meant to human beings from the days of Gilgamesh all the way up to Bambi. Because hunting was originally such a profoundly spiritual activity, and has retained spiritual implications even down to the present day, the book is, not surprisingly, rich with insights into the nature of the human-animal relationship.

For an understanding of the universe of primitive humankind, especially in its relationship to the natural world, the many works of Paul Shepard provide a rich source of ideas, many controversial but all interesting. See especially his *The Others: How Animals Made Us Human* (Island Press, 1997) and *Coming Home to the Pleistocene* (Island Press, 2004). The poet Clayton Eshleman's *Juniper Fuse: Upper Paleolithic Imagination & the Construction of the Underworld* (Wesleyan University Press, 2003) is an adventurous, unorthodox, but extremely rewarding narrative of his decades-long quest to understand the spiritual and psychological underpinnings of Paleolithic cave art, and its insights were a great help to me in writing this book. Joseph Campbell, though often criticized these days for occasional shortcomings in scholarship, remains the most heroically energetic teller of the history of humankind's mythic imaginings, and his writings are full of useful insights into the spiritual aspects of the human-animal relationship. Especially useful is the first volume in his *Masks of God* series, *Primitive Mythology* (Penguin, 1991). David M. Guss's anthology *The Language of the Birds: Tales, Texts, & Poems of Interspecies Communication* (North Point Press, 1986) is an exceptionally rich and useful source of original material, while John Bierhorst's *The Way of the Earth: Native America and the Environment* (William Morrow, 1994) is a masterful survey of specifically Native American ideas and attitudes toward nature.

For those who want to find out firsthand what Christian thinkers from Aquinas to Saint Francis have had to say about the spiritual stature of animals (or their lack thereof), nothing beats Andrew Linzey and Tom Regan's *Animals and Christianity: A Book of Readings* (Wipf & Stock Publishers, 2007). For an in-depth examination of the ins and outs of the biblical view of animals and the implications of that view today, Linzey's *Animal Theology* (University of Illinois Press, 1995) is an excellent source of insights, as are Stephen H. Webb's *On God and Dogs: A Christian Theology of Compassion for Animals* (Oxford University Press, USA, 2002) and Norm Phelps's *The Dominion of Love: Animal Rights According to the Bible* (Lantern Books, 2002). Matthew Scully's powerful and disturbing *Dominion: The Power of Man, the Suffering of Animals, and the Call to Mercy* (St. Martin's Griffin, 2003) is more focused on current issues of animal rights and human responsibilities, but contains many valuable insights into how the modern view of animals, and modern habits of treating and mistreating them, developed over history.

Because of the centrality of nature to Far Eastern spirituality, most books on Eastern religions will have something—and usually quite a lot—to say about the Far Eastern appreciation of nature for its own sake. Daisetz T. Suzuki's classic *Zen and Japanese Culture* (Princeton University Press, 1970), for example, contains lengthy chapters on nature as it appears through the lens of Japanese spiritual thought. For insights into what world religions including but not limited to Christianity have had to say about the spirituality of animals and nature, the works of Seyyed Hossein Nasr are unmatched. See especially his *Religion and the Order of Nature* (Oxford University Press, 1996), and *Man and Nature: The Spiritual Crisis in Modern Man* (Kazi Publications, 2007). *Oriental Mythology*, the second volume of Campbell's Masks of God series, provides much useful material on the Eastern traditions' views of nature, as do many of the works of Mircea Eliade. See especially Eliade's *Patterns in Comparative Religion* (Bison Books, 1996).

Though it took me a while to find them, a number of books on the soul-status of animals actually had been written before the sudden rise in their numbers in the early nineties. In addition to the titles included in the main body of this book, mention should also be made of *Animal Ghosts — A Survey of Animal Extrasensory Perception and Animal Survival of Death* by Raymond Bayless (University Books, 1970), a short but interesting collection that also boasts an introduction by one of the most brilliant investigators of the spiritual implications of paranormal phenomena, Robert Crookall.

NOTES

Introduction

page

1   *"The eyes of an animal"*   Martin Buber, *I and Thou* (Hesperides Press, 2008), 144.

7   *"At the center of our being"*   Thomas Merton, *Conjectures of a Guilty Bystander* (Image Books, 1968), 158.

9   *"something in man (or any other animal)"*   R. B. Onians, *The Origins of European Thought*, 2nd edition (Cambridge University Press), 481.

9   *"the chief designation"*   Ibid.

10   *"We were in a post office"*   Stephen Webb, *Of God and Dogs* (Oxford University Press, 2002), v.

11   *"Children often identify"*   Ibid.

12   *"we need another"*   Henry Beston, *The Outermost House: A Year of Life on the Great Beach of Cape Cod* (Henry Holt, 2003), 24–25.

1. Mystery

19   *"originally lived together"*   "Why Look at Animals?" in John Berger, *About Looking* (Vintage, 1992), 8.

21   *"In the past"*   Ibid., 14.

23   *"A peasant"*   Ibid., 8.

25   *"an animal's blood"*   Ibid., 6–7.

30 *"indistinguishable, each having lost"* Toshihiko Izutsu, *Sufism and Taoism: A Comparative Study of Key Philosophical Concepts* (University of California Press, 1983), 311.

31 *"has two different aspects"* Ibid., 372–73.

42 *"I want to realize"* http://www.mahatma.com/php/showNews.php?newsid=68&linkid=11 (accessed 5/7/08).

45 *"The child-like mind"* The Rev. Canon Callaway, MD, *Nursery Tales, Traditions, and Histories of the Zulus, in Their Own Words* (Trubner and Co., 1868), 135.

47 *"reside in lodges"* Rosalie and Murray Wax, "The Magical World View," *Journal for the Scientific Study of Religion* 1, no. 2 (1962), 181.

48 *"to the primitive"* Lucien Levy-Bruhl, *The Soul of the Primitive* (George Allen & Unwin, 1965), 36.

48 *"It was . . . and still is"* David M. Guss, *The Language of the Birds: Tales, Texts, and Poems of Interspecies Communication* (North Point Press, 1985), ix.

49 *"When addressing animals"* Frank G. Speck, *Naskapi: The Savage Hunters of the Labrador Peninsula* (University of Oklahoma Press, 1977), 72.

49 *"animal souls"* John Bierhorst, *The Way of the Earth: Native America and the Environment* (William Morrow, 1994), 23.

50 *"The creature's body"* Ibid.

51 *"concluded that animals"* Ibid., 21–22.

55 *"According to universal tradition"* Richard Heinberg, *Memories and Visions of Paradise: Exploring the Universal Myth of a Lost Golden Age* (Quest Books, 1995), 75.

58 *"the shaman is supposed"* Mircea Eliade, *Myths, Dreams, and Mysteries* (Harper & Row, 1960), 62.

58 *"We should note"* Ibid., 62–63.

60 *"the earliest members"* Steven Mithen, "The Hunter-Gatherer Prehistory of Human-Animal Interactions," in *The Animals Reader*, edited by Linda Kalof and Amy Fitzgerald (Berg, 2007), 120.

61 *"At present . . . it appears"* Ibid., 121.

62 *"may have been because"* Ibid., 122.

63 *definition of* abstract *New Oxford American Dictionary*, online version, accessed 5/30/08.

64 *"holy occupation"* Calvin Martin, *Keepers of the Game: Indian-Animal Relationships and the Fur Trade* (University of California Press, 1982), 113.

64–65 *"the force which made"* Ibid., 34.

72 *"seated in a typically yogic posture"* Thomas Matus, *Yoga and the Jesus Prayer Tradition* (Paulist Press, 1984), 20.

72 *"Although scholars differ"* Ibid., 21.

75 *"as long as the hunting"* Jan M. Bremmer, *The Early Greek Concept of the Soul* (Princeton University Press, 1983), 129.

76 *"The lord of the animals"* Otto Zerries, from "The Lord of Animals" in *The Encyclopedia of Religion*, vol. 9 (Macmillan, 1987), 22.

76 *"The 'soul' . . . is presumed"* Mircea Eliade, *Shamanism: Archaic Techniques of Ecstasy* (Princeton University Press, 2004), 159.

77 *Khmwum . . . lives "in heaven"* Zerries, "The Lord of Animals," 24.

2. Mastery

79 *"For a long period"* Edward Carpenter, *Pagan and Christian Creeds: Their Origin and Meaning* (Harcourt, Brace and Company, 1921), 223–24.

80 *"humankind was few"* Paul Shepard, *The Only World We've Got: A Paul Shepard Reader* (Sierra Club Books, 1996), x.

82 *"When night had fallen"* Sir James George Frazer, *The Golden Bough: A Study in Magic and Religion: A New Abridgement from the Second and Third Editions*, edited by Robert Fraser (Oxford University Press, 1998), 350.

88 *"probably attracted little"* Richard W. Bulliet, *Hunters, Herders, and Hamburgers: The Past and Future of Human-Animal Relationships* (Columbia University Press, 2005), 136–37.

89 *"The meat from a sacrifice"* Ibid., 121.

92 *"His body was rough"* *The Epic of Gilgamesh*, translated by N. K. Sandars (Penguin Epics, 2006), 2.

93 *"Enkidu ate grass"* Ibid.

93 *"Father, there is a man"* Ibid.

93 *"Extol the strength"* Ibid., 2–3.

93 *"Then, when the gazelle"* Ibid., 4.

101 *"specifically forbade the chewing"* Jan M. Bremmer, *The Early Greek Concept of the Soul* (Princeton University Press, 1983), 125.

103 *"There came to him"* Homer, *The Iliad*, translated by William F. Wyatt; edited by A. T. Murray (Loeb Classical Library, 1924), 23.65–76.

106–7 *"For Plato . . . the soul"* N. T. Wright, *The Resurrection of the Son of God* (Augsburg Fortress Publishers, 2003), 49.

111 *"The hand of the Lord"* Quoted in Olivier Clement, *The Roots of Christian Mysticism*, translated by Theodore Berkeley O.C.S.O. (New City Press, 1993), 217.

111 *"The Greek tradition"* John A. Sanford, *Soul Journey: A Jungian Analyst Looks at Reincarnation* (Crossroad, 1991), 77.

112 *"God has made"* Quoted in Clement, *Roots of Christian Mysticism*, 215.

113 *"the word is present"* Ibid., 218.

113 *"It could even be"* Ibid., 220.

113 *"It may be granted"* Ibid., 220.

114 *"Wisdom . . . consists"* Ibid., 223.

117 *"In Aristotle's view"* Richard Tarnas, *The Passion of the Western Mind: Understanding the Ideas that Have Shaped Our World View* (Ballantine Books, 1993), 61.

120 *"there will be no animal"* Augustine, *The City of God*, translated by Henry Bettenson (Penguin Classics, 2003), 878.

120 *"Because there is in man"* Ibid., 873.

125 *"Matter . . . cannot be destroyed"* E. F. Schumacher, *A Guide for the Perplexed* (Harper Perennial, 1978), 23.

3. The Bridge

131   *"It must be restated"*   Quoted in Mimmo Pacifici, "An important affirmation of John Paul II has raised a great clamor all round the world," http://www.skepticfiles.org/krish/anima.htm (accessed 7/17/08).

131   *"All creatures are balanced"*   Quoted in Kallistos Ware, *The Orthodox Way* (St. Vladimirs Seminary Press, 1995), 45.

136   *"Oh, he's just"*   Jack Becklund, *Summers with the Bears: Six Seasons in the North Woods* (Hyperion, 2000), 21.

137   *"I had just gone"*   Ibid., 158.

138   *"She and Winnie"*   Ibid., 172.

143   *"When Odosha dies"*   Lawrence Sullivan, *Icanchu's Drum: An Orientation to Meaning in South American Religions* (Macmillan, 1990), quoting Marc de Civrieux and David Guss, *Watunna, an Orinoco Creation Cycle* (University of Texas Press, 1997), 161.

145   *"That is our Lord Christ"*   Frank Graziano, *Georg Trakl: A Profile* (Logbridge-Rhodes, 1983), 19.

147   *"He was not well educated"*   M. Jean Holmes, *Do Dogs Go to Heaven? Eternal Answers for Animal Lovers* (Joipax Publishing, 1999), 2.

147   *"The more Mom asked"*   Ibid., 3.

4. The Evidence Grows

157   *"Most of the arguments"*   Louis Agassiz, *An Essay on Classification* (Longman, Brown, Green, Longmans & Roberts and Trubner & Co., 1909), 99.

157   *"Wherever you are going"*   James Herriot, *All Creatures Great and Small* (St. Martin's Press, 1998), 274.

162   *"I was . . . stunned"*   Scott S. Smith, *The Soul of Your Pet: Evidence for the Survival of Animals After Death* (Holmes Publishing Group, 1998), 7.

162   *"As I talked"*   Ibid., 9.

163 *"in the moment"* Aristotle, *On Dreams*, translated by J. I. Beare, http://classics.mit.edu/Aristotle/dreams.html (accessed 6/20/08).

163 *few people "ever pause"* Wilson Van Dusen, *The Presence of Other Worlds: The Psychological/Spiritual Findings of Emanuel Swedenborg*, 2nd edition (Swedenborg Foundation Publishers, 2004), 27.

165 *"He was a beautiful dog"* Smith, *The Soul of Your Pet*, 15.

165 *"beheld the most beautiful sight"* Ibid.

166 *"Bending over the edge"* Eileen J. Garrett, *Adventures in the Supernormal* (Parapsychology Foundation Inc., 2002), 28–29.

170 *"the world and all living beings"* Rupert Sheldrake, *The Presence of the Past: Morphic Resonance and the Habits of Nature* (Park Street Press, 1989), 219.

171 *"Why . . . should matter"* Ibid., 221.

173 *"It was a hauntingly beautiful night"* Bill D. Schul, *Animal Immortality: Pets and Their Afterlife* (Carroll & Graf, 1990), 114–16.

175 *"a universe for which"* Henry Corbin, *Spiritual Body and Celestial Earth* (Princeton University Press, 1989), 78.

176 *"an 'external world' "* Ibid., xxvi–xxvii.

178 *"within the loom"* F. W. H. Myers, narrated through Geraldine Cummins, in *The Road to Immortality: Being a Description of the After-Life Purporting to Be Communicated by the Late F. W. H. Myers Through Geraldine Cummins* (Ivor Nicholson & Watson, Ltd., 1933), 190.

180 *"Mrs. Cady . . . investigated"* Schul, *Animal Immortality*, 113.

181 *"for the dog"* Ibid., 140–41.

183 *"appear to have been great virtuosos"* J. Allen Boone, *Kinship with all Life* (Harper & Brothers, 1954), 7–9.

184 *"Every morning"* Ibid., 52.

184 *"mentally lifting him"* Ibid.

184 *"When we first"* Ibid., 53–54.

185 *"our five organs"* Ibid., 61–63.

185 *"the more I lifted"* Ibid., 64.

186 *"I had spoken"* Ibid., 70–72.

187 *"Let others believe"* J. Allen Boone, *Letters to Strongheart* (Prentice-Hall, 1939), 6.

188 *"I sat up in bed"* Vincent and Margaret Gaddis, *The Strange World of Animals and Pets* (Cowles Book Company, 1970), 221–22.

190 *"If we observe"* Wolfgang Schad, *Man and Mammals: Toward a Biology of Form* (Waldorf Press Publishers, 1977), 1.

190 *"requires the observer"* Ibid., 2.

191 *"This animal"* Ibid., 225–26.

191 *"The cow . . . gazes"* Ibid., 226.

192 *"Death . . . comes to the mouse"* Ibid., 228.

192 *"For the ungulate"* Ibid., 230.

192–93 *"Even when a large"* Ibid.

193 *"Growling horribly"* Ibid.

194 *"A human being"* Ibid., 231.

195 *"Man stands in fact"* Seyyed Hossein Nasr, *Man and Nature: The Spiritual Crisis in Modern Man* (Kazi Publications, 2007), 101.

5. The Return of the Beasts

197 *"One can become"* Nicholas Berdyaev, *The Beginning and the End* (Harper Torchbooks, 1957), 213.

197 *"The dog [is] the animal"* Valentin Tomberg ("Anonymous"), *Meditations on the Tarot: A Journey into Christian Hermeticism* (Tarcher, 2002), 235.

206 *"Friendship . . . is unnecessary"* C. S. Lewis, *The Four Loves* (Harcourt, 1991), 71.

209 *"Christopher Robin . . . was going away"* A. A. Milne, *The Complete Tales and Poems of Winnie-the-Pooh* (Dutton Juvenile, 2001), 326.

211 *"man possesses, in various"* Philip Sherrard, *The Eclipse of Man and Nature: An Enquiry into the Origins and Consequences of Modern Science* (Inner Traditions, 1987), 39.

211 *"All things in creation"* Ibid.

215 *"Man can be"* Ibid., 100.

217 *"I experienced Muri's"* Nicholas Berdyaev, *Dream and Reality: An Essay in Autobiography,* translated by Katharine Lampert (Collier Books, 1962), 20.

219 *"We cannot argue"* Quoted by Reverend. F. O. Morris, B.A., in *Records of Animal Sagacity and Character* (Longman, Green, Longman, and Egberts, 1861), vii.

INDEX

ABOUT THE AUTHOR

Ptolemy Tompkins is the author of *This Tree Grows Out of Hell*, a study of the spiritual underpinnings of the ancient Maya and Aztec cultures of Mesoamerica; *Paradise Fever*, a memoir of growing up with his father, *Secret Life of Plants* author Peter Tompkins; and *The Beaten Path: Field Notes on Getting Wise in a Wisdom-Crazy World*. He is a contributing editor at *Angels on Earth* magazine, and writes a monthly column, "The Winged Life," for Beliefnet.com. His writing has also appeared in *Harper's*, the *New York Times Magazine*, the *Los Angeles Times*, *Time Asia*, *Utne Reader*, *Lapis*, *Best Friends*, *Parabola*, and *Guideposts*.